"Capitalism has collapsed. We are li
Wolff's work is the most importan
questions that are so obvious, the beneficiaries of our out-of-control
inequality don't want them asked. The current failed system has a noose
around all of our necks. Richard Wolff offers an economic vision that gets
our society off the gallows."

- **Jimmy Dore**, American comedian, political commentator, and
author of *Your Country Is Just Not That Into You*

THE SICKNESS IS THE SYSTEM

WHEN CAPITALISM FAILS TO SAVE US FROM PANDEMICS OR ITSELF

Richard D. Wolff

Edited by Liz Phillips & Maria Carnemolla

Published by Democracy at Work
PO Box 30941
New York, NY 10011
info@democracyatwork.info
www.democracyatwork.info

ISBN: 978-1-7356013-0-4

Available through Lulu.com

Cover design by Liz Phillips
This cover has been designed using resources from Flaticon.com

Other Books from Democracy at Work:

Understanding Marxism by Richard D. Wolff

Understanding Socialism by Richard D. Wolff

Table of Contents

Editor's Note

This is a unique collection of essays. We did not want to create a historical retrospective where hindsight is 2020. Thus, this book has been compiled to be a timely guide for analyzing the coronavirus pandemic, the deepening economic crash, dangerously lacking political responses, and exploding social tensions while we are still in their midst.

A book of essays such as this is designed to let the reader choose their own path. It can be read from cover to cover, or picked through for the pieces that are of greatest interest. To help readers navigate their own path, we would like to offer a few points of explanation.

There are five sections to this book. Some themes and points are intentionally repeated because they are relevant in the context of each section, in which essays are ordered by their date of release. The date of publishing adds a pertinent level of understanding of each essay's contents.

Roughly half of this collection are articles by Prof. Wolff originally released in various publications between 2016 and the present. These remain untouched from how they were originally published, and each is attributed to the publication where it first appeared.

The other half of the essays have been adapted from several sources. Many come from sections of episodes of Democracy at Work's show *Economic Update*. Others come from videos on Prof. Wolff's YouTube channel. Some are even reworkings of Prof. Wolff's appearances on other media outlets. These pieces have a much more casual style, something that we wanted to retain as they reflect Prof. Wolff's distinctive ability to explain complex ideas simply.

The blend of formal and colloquial styles that characterizes this mix of essays is intended to provide a relatable and useful read for anyone interested in understanding the current crisis of US capitalism.

With this collection and our other publications, we at Democracy at Work assert that today especially there is an unprecedented and desperate need to do better than capitalism. To move beyond this inherently exploitative, inefficient, and unjust system is no small feat. Regardless of the future developments of this crisis, we feel this book will continue to be relevant to that struggle.

For more information on the sources of these pieces, we invite you to visit the following websites.

From Democracy at Work

Economic Update	www.democracyatwork.info/economicupdate
Wolff Responds	www.youtube.com/RichardDWolff
Ask Prof Wolff	www.youtube.com/democracyatwrk

Publications

Common Dreams	www.commondreams.org
CounterPunch	www.counterpunch.org
Dollars & Sense	www.dollarsandsense.org
Huffington Post	www.huffpost.com
Independent Media Institute	www.independentmediainstitute.org
Economy for All project	
New York Daily News	www.nydailynews.com
Truthout	www.truthout.org

Media Outlets

Letters & Politics	www.kpfa.org/program/letters-and-politics
Loud & Clear with Brian Becker	www.sputniknews.com/radio_loud_and_clear
The Thom Hartmann Program	www.thomhartmann.com
The Zero Hour with RJ Eskow	www.thisisthezerohour.com

Introduction

The COVID-19 pandemic did more than trigger the third capitalist crash in this new century. It also aggravated the dimensions of the crash. The combined pandemic-plus-crash tore away the veneer that had helped people avoid seeing deep social problems and that had allowed politicians repeatedly to evade solutions. The unresolved problems now coalesce into a genuinely epic social crisis. Systemic racism, a badly broken education system, a cash-corrupted politics, ecological degradation — the list of problems becomes clearer and more acute daily. Symptoms of a sick society are everywhere and thus, for many, overwhelming.

The point and purpose of this book is to explain how and why the sickness underlying all those symptoms is the economic system, far more than the viral pandemic. The system is capitalism, and it now faces its greatest crisis ever. Historians remind us how the bubonic plague, or Black Death, provoked the final phase of European feudalism because that pre-capitalist system was already sick with its problems and internal weaknesses. The possible parallel with COVID-19 and global capitalism today is a logical inference that this book explores.

Capitalism has three basic economic problems it has never solved. First, it organizes its enterprises — factories, offices, and stores — undemocratically. A small minority at the top (owners, major shareholders, directors) makes all key decisions impacting employees (the enterprise's majority), but is not accountable to those employees. In societies that enshrine universal suffrage in their politics, and democracy in their governing ideology, the undemocratic hierarchy inside typical capitalist enterprises is a problem. Second, capitalism is unstable. Its business cycles recur, on average, every four to seven years everywhere. They damage and disrupt enterprises, jobs, families, educations, politics, and so on. Third, capitalism generally fosters and deepens inequalities of wealth and income. Capitalism lacks economic democracy, stability, and equality: basic problems.

Across the last several centuries, as capitalism spread from England to its current global prevalence, its three basic economic problems drew the attention of many, both critics and defenders. Various solutions were proposed; some were tried. But none succeeded. When a solution seemed promising, it proved a mirage or, if established, merely temporary. Capitalism's three basic economic problems persisted.

At best, reforms softened the problems' social impacts. Corporations were advised to recognize "stakeholders" beyond their shareholders. Keynes and subsequent economists developed monetary and fiscal policies for governments to use against the system's instability. Such policies moderated business cycles, but only sometimes. They never ended them. And the history of capitalism is filled with efforts to redistribute wealth and income to achieve less inequality. Some efforts succeeded sometimes, but then only temporarily. Most efforts failed. Inequality remains emblematic of today's capitalism in country after country. In the US and beyond, racism (especially directed against black and brown people) repeatedly served to split, distract, and thus weaken working class resistance and opposition to capitalism.

Capitalism has so far outmaneuvered or outlasted the many movements aimed at reforming it. Adroit flexibility and political adjustment have characterized and explained the system's durability. Capitalistic forces even managed to transform the most powerful of global movements against capitalism – socialism – into another version of itself. From a comprehensive opposition to capitalism per se, socialism became instead a movement advocating for the state to control or even replace private capitalists with state officials, and private enterprises with state-operated enterprises. Such were the regimes embodied in the "actually existing socialist societies" over the last century.

The employer-versus-employee structures inside private and state enterprises were, to say the least, remarkably similar. Instability and inequality characterized many kinds of socialism just as they did capitalism, although in different ways and to different degrees. In reality, the "great conflict" of the 20th century – capitalism versus socialism, the US versus the USSR – was predicated on an elaborate mis-specification of what each system actually was. Capitalism, in that great conflict, was *private* capitalism – a system of enterprises producing goods and performing services that were owned and operated by private individuals who occupied no position within a state apparatus. Socialism was *state* capitalism – a system of enterprises either owned and operated by the state and state officials or else privately owned and operated but under direct, intrusive state supervision and regulation. The former socialist structure (one kind of state capitalism) got called "communism," and the latter (another kind of state capitalism) got called "democratic socialism."

The notion of socialism as a basic alternative grounded in enterprises without any employer-versus-employee structure got little attention until the declines of communism and democratic socialism. In recent decades, however, the concept of a socialism that begins with the microeconomic organization of democratic worker cooperatives – where employees are collectively and exclusively their own employer – has increasingly challenged and displaced the older notions.

Both private and state forms of capitalism developed leaders confident that capitalism's three basic economic problems were not existential threats. Critics and protests targeting those problems could safely be ignored, rhetorically placated, or repressed. It seemed unlikely that different social movements demanding the different problems' solutions would coalesce in time, place, focus, and organizational solidarity. Mass media and police were expected to preclude that.

No leader imagined or foresaw what has now happened. The COVID-19 pandemic arrived badly unprepared for. That triggered another of capitalism's periodic crashes. The pandemic and crash worsened one another. Together they triggered social tensions that brought inequality back into the forefront of social consciousness in the US and also beyond. The only economic problem of capitalism that is not exploding before our eyes (yet) is the undemocratic employer-versus-employee enterprise structure. I will return to that at the conclusion of this introduction.

In the essays and updated transcripts of videos and media interviews that follow, readers will find analyses of the intertwined crises of public health and the capitalist economy. The focus is on the United States, but other parts of the world are considered also since both crises were international. Each part of the book targets a different aspect of the intertwined crises. Within each part, essays and transcripts are presented chronologically, as they were produced in response to the crises' evolution.

One consequence of the neoliberalism that took over much of world capitalism after the 1970s was that privatization and deregulation became favored policies for dealing with capitalism's continuous crashes. Authorities thus imposed "austerity measures" after the 2000 dot.com and 2008 subprime-mortgage crises. Public services – including measures to protect and advance public health – and regulations governing private healthcare industries were cut. Those cuts undermined preparations, private and public, for a possible viral pandemic. When COVID-19 hit, it thus triggered the capitalist crash that was already overdue since 2008-2009 (more than the usual four to seven years between crashes). Part I of this book thus argues that the cause of our current societal sickness was not chiefly the virus but rather an unsustainable and vulnerable economic system.

Part II explores capitalism's accumulated vulnerabilities with particular emphasis on how they undermined the capacity to contain COVID-19's spread across the US. The politics and ideology promoted and celebrated by US capitalism had been among its chief supports. In 2020 they became instead agents of glaring failures and decline.

Part III examines how the intertwined pandemic and capitalist crash reawakened millions to social problems capitalism had long been unable to solve. The system had repeatedly "kicked those problems down the road." That is, it deferred seriously addressing what activists demanded in the way of ending racism, unemployment, sexism, poverty, inequality, political corruption, and so on. Pandemic capitalism forcefully returned those problems to the forefront of public awareness. It also intensified them and brought them together as a broad-based, multi-layered challenge to capitalism as a system.

Whenever capitalism has been challenged as a system – and especially when the challenge is as wide and deep as it has been since March 2020 – voices of reform arise. Proposals are made to soften capitalism's harder edges, to reintroduce government regulations dismantled under neoliberalism, to give capitalism a social consciousness, to give the unemployed bigger compensation checks for a while, and so on. Reform proposals also serve as distracting covers for what the main government programs actually do: throw unprecedented amounts of money (via government deficits and central-bank money creation) at capitalists to help them through the crises. Part IV offers critical looks at reforms of capitalism in the past and what that history suggests about the pertinence of similar reforms here and now.

Reforms of capitalism have been achieved mostly in, and because of, its crises. If capitalism's crises were short or shallow enough, capitalists evaded reforms. When reforms were won, they usually proved temporary, as capitalists and their supporters later rolled them back. The so-called COVID-19 crisis of capitalism has provoked proliferating reform proposals. But this time, given the history of past reforms and this latest crisis's extreme severity, reforms may no longer suffice. There are signs that this time reform demands may get swept up into social movements for transition beyond capitalism itself. Such revolutionary movements will define their goals as making sure that the set of changes now arising will not only be achieved but will also endure. Part V considers today's case for, and possibilities of, changing the system as a whole.

All economic systems are born, evolve, and die. As they decline, eventually alternative systems replace them. The catastrophic coincidence of viral pandemic and economic crash places extreme pressure on our institutions and ways of thinking. Over the last three centuries, those have mostly defined and supported the reproduction of capitalism. Yet there were always critical strains of thought and social movements that understood that we can and should do better than capitalism. I hope this book builds on those strains and movements to capture the feeling and thinking of those today who grasp this critical moment in capitalism's history. Like them, it seeks basic economic change as a key part of the way forward.

Part I

Capitalism Crashes Again:
COVID-19 Was Just a Trigger

Exposing Economic Myths: A Low Unemployment Rate, a Fair Minimum Wage and Hourly Pay, and the Greatness of the Market

February 3, 2020
Economic Update: Exposing Economic Myths

There are a number of myths about how the economy in the United States works that deserve to be put aside.

I want to start with the question of employment. This is talked about a great deal these days, because it's one of the very few statistics that Mr. Trump and the Republicans can point to that has at least some positivity to it. We have a low unemployment rate. That is, the percentage of people looking for work who don't find it is relatively small. I don't want to take away from that. But to think that you've understood how the economy is doing – let alone Mr. Trump's boast that it's "great" – after a look at just one statistic is an act of economic incompetence. It's as if you asked a doctor to assess your health, and he told you were healthy after only taking your temperature. You look at many things in order to assess the health of an economy, just like you do with the health of a human being.

For example, one of the reasons the unemployment rate is low is that a lot of people have *given up* looking for work. In the US statistical system, we categorize working people as employed, or unemployed and looking for work, or no longer looking for work. Those no longer looking for work are no longer counted as unemployed. They are considered out of the labor force. As you can see, you need to know that to understand what the numbers mean or don't mean.

Here's another example. Yes, we might have lower unemployment, but suppose that at the same time huge numbers of people went from good jobs with high pay, good benefits, and job security to bad jobs at low pay, no benefits, and no security. This is exactly what's happened over the last decade. What we have done is said to the American people, "You're not going to have good jobs anymore. Here is your choice: no job at all or a job with low pay, no benefits, and little security." Millions of Americans have seen the latter option as more attractive than unemployment. But that's not a sign of economic health, and it sure doesn't mean the economy is great.

Let's look a little further. Back in 1973, the average hourly wage in this country was $4.03 an hour. I did a little calculation that we economists do to take a look at what you could get for $4.03 an hour in 1973 and then adjusted it to 2018 — the last year that we have numbers for. How much money would you need per hour in 2018 to be able to buy the same bundle of goods that you could buy for $4.03 in 1973? You'd need an average of $23.68 an hour. An average wage of $23.68 would be what you'd need for a worker to be able to buy, on average, as much today as he or she could with the average hourly pay in 1973.

Well, what *is* the average wage of the United States in 2018? You need $23.68 to be at the same place you were 50 years ago, but the average today is $22.65. That's right. In America today, in terms of what it can buy, the average wage is *less* than what it was 50 years ago. So, if you're feeling pinched, that your economic situation is difficult, if you've had to adjust your family because living on one person's wage simply will not give you a decent lifestyle, then you are living what has happened.

However, over that same time, your productivity — that's what your labor adds per hour to what your employer produces and sells — that's gone up somewhere in the neighborhood of 25-35 percent. Productivity, your output, what your brains and muscles add to the value of what your employer sells, has gone steadily up. Productivity measures what you, the worker, give to your employer by means of your work. Wages are what the employer gives *you* for *your* work.

Let's review. What the employer has been giving you for the last 50 years has gone nowhere. But what you give to the employer has zoomed up by a third. That's why there's a gap between rich and poor in the United States. Working people, their incomes, have gone nowhere. But the employer class — a small minority in this country — has made out like the bandits that capitalism makes them be.

Next, I'd like to address the minimum wage. In the depths of the 1930s depression, Congress passed a law mandating a federal minimum wage. That law says that employers cannot pay employees less than a certain amount. It's like forbidding capitalists to employ children, or forbidding capitalists to impose themselves sexually on their workers, etc. The minimum wage is a kind of measure of decency in a system.

The current minimum wage is $7.25 an hour, and that's what it's been since 2009. It hasn't been raised in over a decade. Over that time, prices went up every year: one, two, three percent — not a terrible inflation, but they add up over 10 years. The prices have gone up, but the minimum wage hasn't gone up with them, which means, in terms of what the minimum wage can buy, the last 10 years have seen a steady year-by-year decline in what the minimum wage will do for the people – the millions who depend on it.

The minimum wage was the highest, in terms of what it could afford a person earning it, in 1968. Using today's prices, what would our current minimum wage have to be to be comparable to 1968's purchasing power? It would have to be about $12 an hour.

The US has really shafted its people at the bottom. And that's an achievement of the capitalist system, even with a minimum wage. The establishment – having lost its 1930s struggle with workers to create a minimum wage – undermined it in the years afterwards, taking back what they once had been forced to give. It's so bad that a number of states, almost half the states in the union, have higher minimum wages in their states than the federal minimum, because the people in those states have at least understood what an abomination it is to treat people that way. In Washington state, on the West Coast, the minimum wage at the state level is $14 an hour, nearly double the federal minimum. In Washington, D.C., and California it's $13 or more. These states have done what the federal government hasn't done. And let's be clear: The Republicans have been working to keep that minimum wage down. The Democrats – well, the best you can say for them is they haven't been strong enough to do anything other than watch the process unfold.

Next, let me turn to the market. The market is a wonderful institution, we are told. Our leaders keep saying phrases like, "Let the market decide." or "The market will get to the efficient outcome." Really? The market is a very flawed institution that does not deserve the nearly religious kind of endorsement of it that our leaders are eager to provide over and over again. It's time to have a balanced look at the market to evaluate it like every other institution, rather than bow down before it as if we weren't aware of its flaws.

The market economy we live in today has a number of ways of measuring its extraordinary product. I'm going to give you two. The 2,000-odd billionaires in the world today together have more wealth than the bottom half of the population of this planet – three and a half *billion* people. That's right; 2,000 of the richest have more together than the bottom three and a half billion. That's a level of inequality that any system should be deeply ashamed of. Here, in the United States, we even have a better statistic. The *three* richest people have more wealth than the bottom half of the American people. If you think inequality is a problem, then you must understand that it's the capitalist market, which we're supposed to celebrate, that helps produce it.

Many of you are aware of a problem called "gentrification." It's what happens in city after city, neighborhood after neighborhood, as people with money decide they want to live somewhere. They move into that area, buying up homes, paying high rents, so that it becomes impossible for the people who used to live there, who have less money, to stay there. No matter that they grew up there. No matter that their children are going to schools there. No matter that their churches, their friends, and their neighborhoods – none of it matters. Why? Because the *market* is the institution that determines the neighborhood. And if the rich want it, they get it. And the middle and the poor get thrown out. It is something you can see across this country in city after city. It is a sign that we produce not diverse neighborhoods, but the opposite. Over and over again, wealthy people select interesting neighborhoods that they want to live in, they move in, they drive out many of the little businesses, they drive out many of the interesting people, and they end up wondering why they paid so much for a neighborhood that is so dead and so anemic.

It's the market that gentrifies. If we didn't allocate housing according to how much money you have, we wouldn't have the problem of gentrification. It is one of those things markets do that ought to make us very critical. The market is a basic institution that's good for rich people because it favors people with purchasing power.

Imagine a park that's being enjoyed by many families, and the local ice-cream vendor is running out of ice cream. There are 25 children, but there are only six ice creams left. You know what begins to happen in a market economy? The parents who have some money go to the vendor and say, "You know, I know the ice cream costs $3, but I'll give you $5." Other parents, not wanting to be outdone, offer $7. Then some other parents offer $9. As this goes on, the parents who can't afford $9 for an ice cream drop out. And when this process is done, whatever is scarce in an economy goes to the people with the most money. And I ask you, is it ethical? Is it moral? Do you really want to live in a system that takes whatever is scarce and gives it to the people with the most money?

Rural America is dying because there's not enough money there. It's the market that determines that it's not worth it for a bank to locate a branch in a rural area. It's not worth it for a supermarket to go into an area that isn't rich enough. So, people in these areas struggle to get their banking done. They can't get supermarket prices for groceries because they have to pay more at the "convenience store," etc., etc. Because that's how the market works. Rural America is a victim of a market economy.

I'd like to mention something that the markets didn't produce: the middle class, a vast part of the working class who earn enough money to own and live in a house, to have a car, to go on vacation, to send their kids to school. Was this source of American pride created by the market? No. That middle class was created in the depths of the Great Depression, when a revolt from below – the CIO, the socialist and communist parties – created the mass movement that pressured Franklin Roosevelt to do the things that created a middle class: to give millions of people federal jobs, to create Social Security, to pass the first minimum wage, and to create unemployment insurance. These things created the middle class. The market economy resisted it. Capitalists resisted it. The market was the problem, not the solution, for the middle class.

You know why American businesses have closed in the United States and moved to China in huge numbers? That's the market, friends. Nobody forced them. Nobody held a gun to their heads. American corporations wanted to make more profits, which is what they do in a market economy. They could make more profits by going to China, because Chinese workers worked for lower wages there, and because that's a growing economy to sell their goods to. General Motors sells more cars in China than it does here. That's why it's there. Thousands of American corporations decided, following the principles of the market driven by profit, to move. They didn't care about the disaster for American homes, cities, towns, jobs. They were doing what a market capitalism has them do: maximizing profits. The disappearance of jobs here is the product of a market economy.

The Chinese were happy to oblige American businesses, giving them access to their lower-wage workers and to their growing middle class. But in exchange, they wanted to share American technology, and American capitalists agreed. The fact that Mr. Trump now wants to call that "intellectual property theft" is a game that's like paying a bill for something you got and then claiming that the money was stolen from you. And here's the double irony. What is Mr. Trump doing, now that the market has moved production and jobs to China? He's imposing a non-market event – government taxes and tariffs – to try to offset the effects of the market. In his obtuse way, he recognizes that the market is bad news.

That's happened before in American history. In World War II, the American government decided that it couldn't let the market allocate the goods that were scarce then. Production was being used to support the war effort, so much less production went to consumer goods: milk, sugar, meat, gasoline, etc., for civilians. Left to the market, those consumer goods would have gone to rich people because they could bid up and pay the price. Non-rich Americans would have watched in envy and anger. The US government

7

recognized that would destroy the unity you need for war. So, it got rid of the market and substituted a rationing system. Every American got a little ticket book from the government, and to buy milk, sugar, gasoline, meat, etc., you needed a ration ticket. Just having money wouldn't get it for you. The government gave out the ration tickets according to people's needs. If you had a big family, for example, you got a lot of tickets for milk.

These widespread economic myths misrepresent what is going on, and therefore they produce decisions, individuals, corporations, and governments that are not good for what we need in this country at this time. These myths need to be exploded if we are ever to build a more equitable system for the majority of people.

This essay has been adapted from "Economic Update: Exposing Economic Myths" which was published on Democracy at Work's YouTube channel on February 3, 2020.

The Price Gouging of Face Masks

March 2, 2020
Economic Update: When Stale Debates Distract

The coronavirus, a virus that started in Wuhan, China, is rapidly spreading around the world. To limit exposure to the virus, more and more people are wearing masks. An important economics lesson can be learned by this new development. The increased demand for masks has resulted in the prices of these masks skyrocketing in many parts of the world. While the price of a mask was a few dollars before the outbreak, it now can cost ten or even hundreds of dollars, depending on where you live in the world. The technical term for this is "price gouging." A supplier increases the prices of a good to a level much higher than what is considered reasonable or fair, as a result of the increased demand. The reality, however, is that this is simply an example of how markets work.

When something becomes scarce, its availability is minute in comparison to the number of people who want. That's what the word "scarce" means. So, the people producing or selling the objects wanted (in this case, the masks) jack up prices. Either way, the prices rise and so the only people who can save themselves from the virus, insofar as they believe masks will do that, will be those with the most money.

That's how markets work. What is scarce is given to the people with the most money. Is it given to the people who deserve it? To those who need it most? To those who might have waited the longest for it? To the people whose respiratory systems make them most vulnerable to a virus? To those whose age or work activity puts them more at risk? No; it's given to the people with the most money.

There's really no morality to this. A governmental authority, particularly a democratic one, should distribute scarce things in a way that respects people's democratic decisions about the community's needs for scarce materials. But that's not how markets work. They're anti-democratic.

What defense do pro-market economists come up with? Many, including some of my colleagues, say that, when prices go up, profits go up, too, and that incentivizes companies to produce these masks. I look incredulously at my colleagues at the naivete of this. I say to them: "What are we supposed to do while we wait for the suppliers to produce more? In the meantime, we're giving the surplus to the people who are richest, and we're screwing everybody else. What kind of a system does that?"

But here's the more important point: Suppliers know this logic. They've taken the same economics course you have, and they know that they can make more money holding *back* on the increase of supply than if they rush out there as if they were textbook robots producing more. Why bother producing more? It's risky. The virus may disappear or the cure might be found. It's deemed much smarter to grab the money quickly by letting prices rise, and that's how it usually works. There is no good defense for how markets allocate scarce goods. When it's a life-or-death situation as with the coronavirus, that lesson really needs to be learned. It's long overdue.

This essay has been adapted from "Economic Update: When Stale Debates Distract" which was published on Democracy at Work's YouTube channel on March 2, 2020.

US Health System Colludes with Pandemic

March 23, 2020
Economic Update: Comedy and Tragedy of Capitalism

Let me begin by indicating what some of the problems are that a capitalist medical system, of the sort we have in the United States, presents when dealing with something as big as the coronavirus pandemic.

On one hand, 30 million Americans have no medical insurance. This means they don't go to the doctor when they have something they think is a passing flu, viral or bacterial, because they can't afford to pay the astronomic cost that confronts someone without insurance. Likewise, for such a person to go to the emergency room (which would be an option under other circumstances), becomes something you don't want to do in the face of a crisis. This is especially true because if there are likely to be people infected by this virus, you're going to find them in an emergency room!

On the other hand, 100 million Americans have insurance, but with such high deductibles and/or sizable co-pays that they don't have the money to cover them. They will hesitate to be tested, and therefore they will spread the disease (if they have it) in ways that a properly designed health insurance program could reduce. Millions more Americans have no paid sick leave from their job, so they will stay at their job as long as possible. We also have many undocumented immigrants, afraid of going to any medical facility because, beyond financial risks, it will subject them to dangers from ICE or other immigration authorities.

All together, this is a collection of people so molded by our medical profit system that, for no fault of their own, are colluding with this epidemic. They don't want to, but the system forces it on them.

We also have a law in the United States that allows mandatory quarantining of people, but it doesn't cover the costs of a quarantine when a person loses his or her income. This is crazy. If you quarantine people who have the disease, and you will not cover the cost of it, you give them an incentive to not be tested and to avoid quarantine. The Trump administration has recently made statements about tax relief and aid for airlines and travel companies affected by this crisis. Once again, we see where the priorities in a capitalist system lie: with the corporations and not the mass of people whose health is threatened.

To give you an idea of how things could be otherwise, I'm going to pick one country: South Korea. The epidemiological situation there is more extreme than ours in the United States at the time of writing. South Korea has a universal health insurance program. On top of that, coronavirus testing is free for every single person in South Korea, and that includes immigrants who are specifically guaranteed that no information about their treatment will be shared with any other governmental institution. You do not have to be a South Korean citizen to get the free testing. Yet, in the United States, a much richer country, nothing like that is being done.

And then we have the market system, our proud market system, that is distributing scarce testing kits, scarce masks and scarce equipment to people who *can* pay. That's right. If you have a lot of money, you can go on to the Internet and find these rare healthcare items. They are distributed according to how much money you have, not according to what your need is. Medical personnel need to be safe in treating those who come for testing. They obviously should be the first in line for getting the equipment and anything else that might help. But not in a market system, where instead it goes first to those with the most money.

On March 8th, the New York Times regaled us with a list of all the things rich people are doing to escape the virus: the yachts that they are moving on to, the bunkers they have created on their property to hide in, the expensive masks that they are able to get worth hundreds or even thousands of dollars. It's charming to watch how the system works. In the United Kingdom, the Competition and Markets Authority is monitoring the situation and may ask the government to impose price controls. In other words, there is recognition, at least in the UK, that the market as an institution fails at dealing with similar situations. And as you know from our show "Economic Update," it isn't very good at dealing with many other things, either.

This essay has been adapted from "Economic Update: Comedy and Tragedy of Capitalism" which was published on Democracy at Work's YouTube channel on March 23, 2020.

Coronavirus: A Capitalist Crisis

March/April 2020
Dollars & Sense.

Consider the gross failure of the U.S. private, profit-driven, capitalist medical- industrial complex (four industries: doctors, hospitals, drug and device makers, and medical insurance firms). They decided not to prepare for a serious virus problem. Will so huge a failure finally tip U.S. ideology and politics in favor of socializing health care? Will the parallel preparatory failure of the U.S. government, long captured by its corporate donors in general and those in the medical-industrial complex in particular, boost a resurgent U.S. socialism? Or will a traumatized, socially distanced population turn rightward instead to a dictator for salvation from a clearly out-of-control crisis?

Trump, his government, and the system he serves need to blame the Corona catastrophe in the United States on something other than U.S. capitalism. Enter the Trump/GOP nationalism that generally scapegoats foreigners (immigrants, trading partners, etc.). Official blame targets what Trump calls "the Chinese virus."

Yet such blaming is racist, divisive, and ignorant. Viruses have always been part of our natural world. Ongoing mutations have repeatedly produced strains that have caused widespread human sickness and death. That is why medical science has long studied viruses. In the 1918 flu epidemic, the H1N1 virus killed almost 700,000 in the United States plus many millions more around the world. It began in Kansas, yet no one since called it "the U.S. virus." H1N1 resurfaced in 2009 as "swine flu." Other recent viruses include SARS (2002–2004) and MERS (since 2012).

Given that history of viruses, systematic preparation for future outbreaks of seriously dangerous viruses was an obvious social need. Availability of sufficient (many millions of) tests was needed for the crucial role of identifying and separating the infected from the uninfected. Producers of ventilators, masks, hospital beds, etc. should have stockpiled them. Training should have been routinized to equip more than enough volunteers to help cope with outbreaks. To block disease transmission, plans should have been made to accommodate social distancing: securing suitable locations, appropriate supervision, distribution of supplies, etc. Likewise, the consequences of social distancing—lost jobs, closed businesses, disrupted supply chains, crippled purchasing power, chaotic credit markets, etc.—should have been planned for. The newly unemployed could and should have been re-employed to manage social distancing. Yet no remotely adequate planning occurred.

U.S. capitalism failed at everything on this partial list of "shoulds." Capitalist industries failed to serve public health because private profits were an inadequate incentive for them to do so.

The government failed to compensate for private capitalism's failures, as usual, because government leaders (drawn heavily from corporate CEO ranks) share similar mentalities.

Knowledge of the dangerous new coronavirus emerged clearly from China in December 2019. CDC documents from this past January show full awareness of its huge threat and of China's extreme social distancing measures undertaken to control it. China's massive coordination of public and private resources saw profits displaced by public health as the prioritized goal or "bottom line." South Korea acted similarly. In contrast, neoliberalism has arisen and prevailed in many countries since the 1970s. It undermined the state by privatizing and deregulating. Such steps blocked the kinds of social mobilization achieved in China and South Korea. Social mobilization was and remains more partial, fragmentary, and slower in Italy, the United States, and beyond.

When infections and deaths mounted quickly, panic followed. Political leaders saw threats to their positions. Most people began to grasp how misled and underprepared their nations were, that their jobs, income, and lives were in danger. They saw their leaders floundering atop an out-of-control situation. As debt-ridden economies collapsed into sharp recessions or worse, corporate leaders turned, as usual, to the state for bailouts even as global capitalism still shook from the results of the 2008–2009 bailouts.

Crisis moods overtake most of us as we watch desperate leaders' evident failures to cope. Schools are shut, but without plans to handle consequences: children not taken care of, taught, or often not even fed; parents with children now at home who cannot continue their jobs; emotional strains on families thrown together. No plan exists to train mental health counselors to help work on these problems. Panicked leaders foresee a possible unemployment rate of 20% (it was 25% in 1933) yet also propose cash distributions of $1–2,000 per taxpayer. That laughably inadequate response typifies what one has come to expect from a government that failed to stockpile tests, masks, and hospital beds.

Either public health—including preparedness for viruses—dominates private profit for capitalists or it does not. The coronavirus catastrophe demonstrates the results when public health is subordinate to private profit and to a governmental apparatus that adulates the superiority of private over public administration.

History's latest virus, the coronavirus, has threatened and challenged U.S. society. But it has been our political economy that failed to meet the challenge, to defeat the threat. The catastrophe we are living through was caused by a capitalist system that could not anticipate, plan for, or cope with the coronavirus. To "get through" this catastrophe (as we did with the 1930s depression) yet leave the system intact will guarantee the next catastrophe. The need for a different economic system and a different government responsible to it is the lesson we need to learn now. Doing so can yield something positive amid the mammoth negatives raining down on us.

This article was published in the March/April 2020 issue of Dollars & Sense.

Capitalism is too Inefficient to Handle Coronavirus Pandemic

April 4, 2020
Wolff Responds

I'm in a remote location trying to be safe as I know all of you are trying as well. This is a difficult time, but it is also a time when we can learn very valuable lessons that will go far beyond the pandemic that oppresses us now.

One of the lessons to be learned from the virus is the utter inefficiency of capitalism. It has exposed this to us in a stunning way that requires some close attention; because what is true about capitalist inefficiency during the coronavirus pandemic is true all the time. Let me explain.

The inefficiency of capitalism in the face of the coronavirus is simple. We know about viral pandemics. We have experienced several over the last half century. They come from time to time, they can be devastating, they have to be controlled so they don't spread from one person to another, etc. We know all that. Our scientists know it. Our medical system knows it. In the face of a well-known danger that periodically recurs, the only rational, efficient human response is to prepare, to plan, and to have ready the means to minimize death, sickness, damage and loss. The US should have produced the test kits, masks, ventilators, hospitals, beds, gowns, and other necessary protective gear. We should also have had a plan for social distancing in our schools, workplaces, etc.

But capitalism is a system focused on profits— profits for the enterprise and profits as soon as possible for the enterprise. We fetishize profits in a capitalist system, and it is a kind of disease. So, none of this preparation was done because it wasn't profitable. It's not profitable for a company to make ventilators in large numbers and then to stockpile them for uncertain sale in the future. That's too risky, a loser for a profit system. Ditto for hospital beds, face masks, you name it. Capitalism is a system that makes people do what is profitable.

We have now lost so much wealth and human life, with a value that is substantially more than it would have taken to prepare and act adequately. Capitalism wasn't "efficient." It was horrifically, inhumanely inefficient. It failed to prepare us for the costs of the pandemic, and this is not unique.

Capitalism's profit motive is not efficient and it never was. The capitalist argument is: it's not "efficient" to provide affordable housing for everybody.

16

What does that mean? It's not profitable! If you took houseless people and you provided them with jobs they could do, incomes they could earn, and housing they could afford, the benefits to our society would be enormous. But we don't do that. Not only is that the efficient thing to do, it's also the only humane thing to do. But capitalism is not efficient in dealing with the houselessness problem, or with the coronavirus. Capitalism is a system that puts profits ahead of everything else—and that includes efficiency. No one should worry that a transition from capitalism to socialism, or some other post-capitalist society would compromise efficiency.

Capitalism does lots of horrifically inefficient things. That alone is a reason to be far more open to a better system, one that deals with the efficiency question head-on. Pursuing profits doesn't magically get us efficiency. It's not doing it now, and it never did.

This essay has been adapted from "Wolff Responds: Lessons Learned from Corona Pandemic" which was posted on Professor Wolff's YouTube channel on April 4, 2020.

COVID-19 Was a Trigger, But Capitalism Caused the Economic Crash

April 17, 2020
Truthout

After the dot-com crash in 2000, economic policy aimed to "get us back to normal." It sought to recreate or re-establish the U.S. economy as it was before the crisis hit. After the subprime mortgage crisis, economic policy likewise proceeded to "recovery." That meant returning to how the economy was before 2008-2009. Now, as we sink into an economic depression by reacting so poorly to the coronavirus, Federal Reserve and Trump Treasury policies seek to return us to that "great economy" Trump boasted about before March 2020.

The repeated policy flaw lay in not grasping the basic problems of the U.S. capitalist economy before each of the three crashes dogging the first two decades of the new century. Those problems were key contributors to those crashes, more important than the events that triggered them. We should not be fooled by the desperate efforts of capitalism's defenders who name crashes after their triggers, which just distracts attention from how and why capitalism's vulnerabilities helped turn triggers into crashes. Policy aimed to return U.S. capitalism to its status quo ante each crash only guaranteed passage straight into the next crash.

Tendencies toward ever-greater inequality and instability have haunted capitalism throughout its history. Capitalism's leaders and ideologues therefore tried everything they could think of to end, tame and distract from those tendencies that periodically threatened the system itself. Against inequality, capitalism experimented with progressive tax structures, minimum wages, redistributive schemes, welfare states, universal basic incomes, and so on. Yet, as Thomas Piketty's work shows, capitalism's tendencies to perpetuate greater inequality persist. Periodically, when mass uprisings against inequality succeeded in stopping or even reversing those tendencies, the stoppages or reversals proved temporary.

Against its likewise intrinsic instability, capitalism has repeatedly tried Keynesian monetary and fiscal policies plus all sorts of reforms, regulations, stabilizers, and so on. However, all failed to stop capitalism's business cycle, the system's recurring accumulation of imbalances and weaknesses culminating in sharp declines (crashes) in employment, production and economic activity generally. The events that trigger each capitalist crash differ as do specific features distinguishing one crash from another. However, the role of the capitalist system itself in periodically reproducing crashes is glaringly evident in the historical record.

Before the coronavirus hit the U.S. in March 2020, our economic system was not "great," as Trump boasted during his re-election efforts. The corporate sector was lumbering under an immense load of accumulated debt. As the crashes of 2000 and 2008 had ushered in Federal Reserve policies reducing interest rates, U.S. businesses of all sizes found they could borrow limitless monies at historically low interest costs. Borrowing became the easiest and cheapest way to solve each and every business problem that arose. Thus, monetary policies to try and cope with one capitalist crash helped set in motion responses building to the next crash. By closing businesses down, the coronavirus stopped the profits that enabled accumulated corporate debts to be paid. Defaults then undermined and froze credit markets that traded securitized corporate debt, the derivative instruments insuring that debt and those securities, and so on.

The U.S. economy before COVID-19 hit was also home to a private, capitalist medical-industrial complex. Private profit calculations led firms in that complex decision to not produce or stockpile the masks, tests, ventilators, beds, etc. needed to combat a pandemic. The U.S. government, staffed and ideologically controlled by leaders borrowed from the corporate sector, did not compensate for the private sector's failure to produce or stockpile what was needed for a dangerous virus. Efficiency in generating profits trumped efficiency in securing public health. Losses in wealth since March 1, 2020, far exceed the costs of producing and stockpiling needed supplies to contain and combat the virus. Capitalism's profit-driven decisions proved monumentally inefficient.

Trump's "great economy" had worsened the income and wealth inequalities that existed in 2016. Obama's government presided over deepening inequalities too. These inequalities constrained mass consumer purchasing power and that in turn constrained investment in production. The Fed's new money creation and record low interest rates in the post-2008 "recovery" brought stock price inflation to the stock market. The exploding distance between the stock market and the underlying economy of goods and services production accumulated an imbalance (bubble) just waiting for a trigger to unravel (burst).

The post-2008 recovery lasted longer than the average such period (four to seven years historically) after a capitalist crash. Longer-than-average periods usually meant that the next crash (what we are in now) would be worse than the average crash (as it is now). The post-2008 recovery also witnessed extreme measures to avoid any basic changes in the capitalist system. For example, efforts to re-establish some version of the Glass-Steagall Act (a banking reform in the wake of the 1929 crash) were successfully resisted, watered-down and delayed by the big private banks. This helped return the economy to its pre-2008 economy "normal." With Trump's arrival in 2016, that return to normal became a rush backwards to an ever-less regulated private capitalism. All these developments helped steer the economy toward its next crash now.

To cope with the current crisis, massive direct interventions to transform the economy are needed. In the first place, a massive relief program — patterned on the relief programs developed in the 1930s Great Depression — is needed. Bernie Sanders has developed a solid outline for doing that. Beyond relief (and just as important), production and distribution need to be reorganized to respect conditions of social distancing alongside ongoing medical testing and monitoring of a threatened population, and monitoring of all populations immediately upon outbreaks of new, dangerous viruses anywhere in the world. Public health must be the priority — far more important than private profits and employer interests. The resulting economy will be very different from — and in many ways, a challenge to — the economy that existed before March 2020.

Because the shared dominant policy goal of Trump, the Republicans and the Democrats aims to return to a pre-virus "normal," what needs to be done was not and is not being done. Employers did not and do not now want to pay the costs of making workplaces safe against coronavirus, yet they want employees back on the job as they were before the pandemic. That goal is not only dangerous to our health in this pandemic, it is also a direct economic threat. The U.S. establishment's preferred policies prioritize returning to a capitalist economy with immense, dangerous weaknesses over serving public health now. Those bipartisan establishment policies respond to the current crash in ways that launch capitalism toward its next crash.

This article was published by Truthout on April 17, 2020.

Before COVID-19, We Were Already Due for a Crash

April 28, 2020
Wolff Responds

Toward the end of April, it's now clear that we're going to have somewhere between 30 and 40 million people filing for unemployment. Let's remember that this is already, not only the greatest crash since the Great Depression of the 1930s, but the official unemployment rate underestimates the reality. It does not consider the 10 to 12 million undocumented immigrants in the United States. Many of them will have also lost their jobs, but cannot file for unemployment. Most are afraid to go anywhere near government agencies for fears of being captured by Immigration and Customs Enforcement (ICE) and deported.

This is a collapse of enormous significance, and I want to challenge the notion that this crash is first and foremost about the coronavirus. It isn't. What do I mean?

Capitalism is a three-to-four-hundred-year old economic system. It is thought to have begun, at least in its modern form, in England back in the 17th century. Capitalism took off from England to the rest of Europe, North America, Japan and beyond. Now it's our global economic system. Here is the single most important fact about this system's history: wherever capitalism settled in as the major dominant economic system, it crashed every four to seven years. Every four to seven years, suddenly significant numbers of people lose their jobs; and it's not because they don't work as well as they did before, or because they aren't as productive as they were before. It has nothing to do with the individual worker. The system itself breaks down. The employer suddenly can't sell what the enterprise produces, and so it lays off employees. Those laid-off people lose their income and buy less things. So other employers can't sell their goods, which means they lay off their workers. It's a downward spiral that we call a recession, a depression, a downturn, a crash, a crisis. We have so many words for this.

In studying capitalism's history, we know that this happens every four to seven years. Sometimes, the economic crashes are short-lived and don't cut very deep. But other times, they cut very deep and last for a long time. The Great Depression of the 1930s hit in October 1929 and it really didn't end until early 1941. That's 11 long years. The Great Depression was a capitalist downturn that was long and deep. They often can be like that.

The last one we had was in 2008-2009. It was another deep crash, almost as bad as the Great Depression, and got the name the Great Recession.

We're now in the year 2020. In the first 20 years of a new century, we've had three economic crashes. The first one (spring 2000) got the name "dot-com crash." The share prices of several high-tech companies skyrocketed, even though these companies were young and had never earned a profit. Eventually, buyers of these high-priced shares panicked and sold them. Those share prices tanked and took the broader market down too. However, that crash didn't cut too deep and it didn't last too long. Then in 2008-2009 we had another, the "subprime mortgage crash." It was pretty much on schedule. This one was big, it cut deep, and it lasted a long time. It started in the middle of 2007 and wasn't done until well into 2010.

Now, in 2020, the crash is being called the "coronavirus crash". Notice how the names are given not to a capitalism that crashes every four to seven years, but rather to whatever sets it off? The trigger in 2000: dot-com stock prices. In 2008: people failing to pay mortgages. In 2020: a virus. Well, I think it's illegitimate to call these crashes by what triggers them. They ought to be called what they are: the endlessly recurring crashes of an unstable capitalist system.

Do the arithmetic. To have three crashes in the last twenty years works out to be, on average, every seven years. If it hadn't been for those particular triggers, it would have been something else. How do I know? Because for three to four hundred years, it was always something else. It's true that each crisis is unique and it has its unique trigger and condition. But the recurring pattern is something you have to face: capitalism is an unstable economic system that crashes every four to seven years. A level of instability like that is an enormously important reason to be critical of this system and to try, with others, to make a transition to a better system.

From the beginning, leaders and defenders of capitalism have been trying to overcome its every four-to-seven-year crash pattern. They've tried everything, including government monetary and fiscal policies of all kinds. In the 1930s, we even had a new economic model developed by a British economist, John Maynard Keynes. We now call this Keynesian economics, and it focuses on how to stop or manage these crashes. But so far, nothing has been found to stop capitalism's crashes. That is why we are in one now.

If you lived with a person as unstable as capitalism, you would have moved out long ago.

We have a system that doesn't work for most people. It produces grotesque inequality, it is unstable, and it has proven incapable of securing our safety during a global pandemic. This virus came at a time when we should have and could have known that our economic system was vulnerable to crashes. Make no mistake, blaming the virus for this crash muddles the issue. The problem is the system.

This essay has been adapted from "Wolff Responds: The System is the Problem not Virus" which was posted on Professor Wolff's YouTube channel on April 28, 2020.

Those Who Say They Know When the Crisis Will End Are Pulling Your Leg

June 12, 2020
Loud & Clear with Brian Becker

The first time the unemployment numbers went down Mr. Trump made a mountain out of this really small molehill in order to make his presidency look anything other than the disaster it is. But in April and May, with skyrocketing unemployment numbers, Mr. Trump finally could say nothing about how well the economy was doing.

But I want to clarify something that has been misreported. The unemployment rate for April and May of 2020 was announced at a little over 13%. However, there was a footnote that said the Bureau of Labor Statistics (BLS) *did not count* people who said their status is "temporary" as unemployed.

Normally the opinion of the unemployed person is neither solicited nor taken seriously because the question is: "Are you working, or are you not?" Your notion of how long you'll be out of work may be interesting for other purposes beyond macroeconomic statistics. Nevertheless, if the BLS *had* counted the people mentioned in their footnote, the unemployment rate would have been 16.5%. And that still would have been low, since it does not count all of the undocumented immigrants, millions of them in this country, who lost their jobs. To discuss the unemployment statistics and ignore these facts is not only misreporting, but lying by omission.

Unemployment is terrible, and it has reached a level we had never imagined we would see again after the Great Depression. This is not going away anytime soon despite what the public relations machine of the extreme right in this country (including the President) might say. We are in the early stages of this crash and we're not even fully aware yet of what is going to happen.

Consider the commercial rent crisis. If the landlords win their legal battles and squeeze their commercial tenants for rent, there is going to be a further increase in unemployment because many of those tenants are going to go out of business. On the other hand, if the tenants win over the landlords, the outcome might not be quite so bad for unemployment. But which side will win these mounting legal battles is unclear.

So, the glib notion that we're going to be out of the woods as of September, December, or next March is worthless speculation of people who, if they're honest with you, don't know. With economic downturns we never know how deep they will go and how long they will last. That is even more true now because this crash is so much bigger and happening at the same time as a global pandemic hits the world. This makes predicting long-term unemployment a fool's game.

In June, the Congressional Budget Office (CBO) revised a January projection, now calculating that the US economy will grow by 7.9 trillion dollars less from 2020 to 2030 than what it had previously projected. This quick recalculation gives you an idea of what these predictions are worth. It would be fine to not know the unknowable as long as you put a footnote or asterisk there and you explain to people what assumptions you've made. But the uncertainty torments people, so when they ask questions there are always people who offer "answers."

There's a tremendous conflict going on about how to react to all of this and that is now being fought out in every enterprise, in every industry. We have no idea which ones are going to come back. We don't know whether restaurants are going to be a business we read about in history books the way we read about other ancient phenomena that no longer exist. The lack of clarity, the lack of any touchstone that will give us a clear idea is one of the most important things to keep in mind as we go ahead.

This essay has been adapted from an appearance of Professor Wolff's on the program Loud & Clear with Brian Becker which aired on June 12, 2020.

Dark Times, Hard Truths

June 17, 2020
Economic Update: Dark Times, Hard Truths.

A devastating lack of preparedness in response to both the coronavirus and the economic crash well demonstrates how capitalism has failed at managing these twin, overlapping crises.

The overwhelming failure we're experiencing is the failure to test the population. We haven't tested the vast majority of American people, and it's a disaster that this system has yet to provide for it. Ample and accurate testing is crucial to giving workers and consumers the confidence necessary to reopen America. This problem is underscored when the President, or any employer, is seen on television urging or even threatening people to go to work while being silent on any demand or mandate that the employer provide a safe and healthy workplace.

But the failure goes beyond that. A story recently in the *Los Angeles Times* speaks about the "Wild West" of virus testing companies. If you read the story, you will learn that there are many companies trying to jump on the testing bandwagon in various ways. Here's what that means—profit is the driver. All these companies want to profit from Americans who desperately want to be tested, because the system has failed to test them to this point. The article reports on employers buying wildly overpriced testing equipment not knowing whether that equipment will produce reliable test results or even work at all.

Instead of a coordinated national focus on solving this problem by giving priority to testing, we leave the market to solve the problems it helped create in the first place. We allow profit-driven companies to produce and market who knows what in the way of testing. And when some of these tests turn out to be false or unreliable then we're going to have people who don't get tested, because they don't believe there's a point in it. The problem worsens itself. This is a failure to manage a social problem, and it is a capitalist failure—that's what must be understood.

To add to the list of capitalism's failures, in response to the most recent economic crash the Federal Reserve has decided to purchase more corporate debt. This means that if you are a company and you borrow money in the market, you give the lender (who gives you the money) a certificate called a corporate bond. That bond is your promise as a corporation to repay that loan at a certain point, with interest, over the time between now and then. Here is what is happening now. The corporations

26

go into the market and borrow the money. They have no trouble finding the lender. Why? Because now when the lender gives the corporation the loan (and receives the bond) the lender immediately, often within seconds, sells that bond to the Federal Reserve for money that the Fed creates from nothing.

The banks started with the money, they lent it to the corporation, they got the bond, they sold the bond to the Federal Reserve, and now they have more money than they started with 25 seconds ago. They've made a nice little piece of change too. They do this over and over again.

Every large company in the country can borrow huge amounts of money this way now. You may be suffering as an unemployed person (one of the 40 million), your company may be small and going out of business, but if you're big enough to issue bonds—there's no limit. Inequality between big versus medium and small businesses will get worse in the United States as a result of this. Corporations will load up on even more debt than they have now. This is a situation getting worse, not better.

On top of this, half of all commercial rents weren't paid in May. Almost as many weren't paid in April. Commercial renters are actually not paying their rents at a higher rate than residential renters. In other words, the capitalists who always tell us that private property is sacrosanct, that contracts cannot be violated, are in fact violating their leases and their contracts for the space they occupy. Landlords are, therefore, in difficulty. What the landlords will do now is fight back.

They're not getting any money from their tenants so they can't pay back the banks from whom they borrowed the money to develop the mall, store, or whatever it is that they're leasing to the commercial tenant. It's a situation spiraling out of control, and it has serious ramifications because commercial loans have been packaged into securities in just the way that mortgages were that led to the crash of 2008 and 2009.

As a result, the courtrooms are full of disputes. Landlords are filing suits against the stores who aren't paying rent, dozens of them every day, all across the United States. Banks are even beginning to sue the landlords who aren't paying back their loans. The people who invested in those securities, those counting on commercial loans to be repaid, are not going to see their money. They will surely sue as well. Millions of companies have been unable to honor all kinds of contracts because of the pandemic, because of the crash, and because the government has handed out money based on political considerations and not based on the underlying economic reality. It is chaotic and will breed more chaos, not just because

27

of the problems with the pandemic, but also with how the capitalist system is being used and abused to treat them.

It's unclear who will win, but here's the point. If you're rich enough to hire the best lawyers, you'll win this one and you'll screw those who are less wealthy, who can less afford lawyers and all the rest. It's what the French call "*sauve qui peut*"—everyone for themselves.

If the working class doesn't get itself together and mobilize its resources and its people, it will come out on the short end of this game because everybody else is lawyering up to fight out who gets screwed and who gets saved. The reason people joined labor movements in the 1930s—the greatest moment of labor union organizing in American history—is because they understood that this is a struggle in which your numbers and the resources you can tap will determine how you come out at the end. Capitalism does not manage its own failures very well. And it's very dangerous to get caught up in those failures without organization to give you the strength you cannot manage on your own.

This essay has been adapted from "Economic Update: Dark Times, Hard Truths" that aired on Democracy at Work's YouTube channel on June 17, 2020.

Part II

Capitalism versus COVID-19:
Failures to Prepare, Contain, or Both

How US Politics Sustains US Capitalism

August 19, 2018
Common Dreams

Until their contradictions explode coexisting economic and political systems sustain one another. "Normal" politics includes precisely the process of working out social conflicts such that the economic system is sustained. Whatever its form, the state's tasks include that sustenance. When politics and the state can no longer perform adequately, the system totters. Only then can movements for system change seriously contest the existing system and press for transition to another.

Capitalism displays this pattern in general and particularly in the United States. To see this, we divide the US population into three groups. The first comprises the 1% richest, mostly corporate directors, etc. The second is the 9% below them who are mostly professional assistants and servants to the 1%. Below them, the third group includes 90% of the population split between the poorest 45% and the remaining 45%. (henceforth the "middle"). The top 10% are the dominant funders, leaders, etc. of both major parties, Republican (R) and Democrat (D). Separately and in comfortable oscillation, both parties sustain US capitalism.

The Ds loudly sympathize with and appeal to the bottom 45%. Those millions get paid poorly, have few benefits, and suffer job insecurity. Because they have relatively little to lose, they represent a constant potential threat to capitalism. To counter that threat, the Ds support policies to soften the system's hard edges: minimum wages, progressive tax structures, welfare supports, etc.

Left Ds want the top 10% to pay for those policies. Moderate or centrist Ds disagree. They fear that such an approach risks driving otherwise sympathetic members of the top 10% to redirect financial, media, and other resources from D to R. With few, temporary exceptions, moderate Ds have prevailed. Thus, when D's policies govern, their tax costs fall heavily on with maximum effect on the middle.

The Rs work differently. They stress that D policies are chiefly driven by concern for the bottom 45%. They underscore the unfairness of taxing the "hard workers" in the middle to fund the bottom 45%, the "takers." Rs often characterized those "takers," often in racialized terms, as unwilling to work hard or at all, dependent on the nanny state, etc. Rs describe their political goal as ending the "special" benefits for the bottom 45% ("except for the truly needy") and thereby saving taxpayers in the middle. The Rs' rhetoric keeps the top 10% happy because it proceeds as if the political struggle (e.g., over taxes) is only between the two halves of the bottom 90%. When left Ds discuss raising taxes on the top 10%, Rs dismiss such talk as "class war" and utterly unrealistic.

While both parties readily describe themselves as capitalist or pro-capitalist, it is especially their oscillation in office that sustains capitalism. The policies of one party proceed until they so aggravate the country that demands for "change" arise. That demand is met by moving to the other party and its policies. System criticism and system change stay out of politics.

R's insist that deregulating and subsidizing "job-creating" capitalists will trickle down to benefit all. The Ds propose helping especially the bottom 45% because trickle down happens too little and too late. When Ds win, resentment builds and opens the way for Rs to oust Ds and proceed to cut social services for the bottom 45%. Trump is well within this oscillating tradition although he won by positioning himself outside and against the mainstream Ds and Rs. That tapped the mass rage built up against both as responsible for the ever-greater distance between the top 10% and all the rest.

Today establishment Ds again urge the bottom 45% to reject the extremity of Trump's administration. That—plus the usual salacious revelations, corruptions, etc.—may win over "moderate" Rs alienated by the Trump spectacle. If another oscillation empowers the Ds in 2018 and/or 2020, US politics will again sustain the capitalist system. D's would likely repress both independent movements for system change (as Obama crushed Occupy Wall Street) and moderately parallel movements inside their party.

Of course, contradictions beset all relationships including that linking US politics and US capitalism. Politics always also undermines, as well as sustains, capitalism. Which effect prevails depends on how the myriad of social influences shapes the relationship. For example, the state has always undermined capitalism by the potential threat it presents. Given universal suffrage, the state's dependence on majority voting always risks producing state policies that hurt capitalism or even end it by moving instead to, say, socialism or feudalism, etc. That is why laissez-faire and libertarian ideas have always been fostered by capitalism. They work to keep the state weak, hobbled, demonized, etc.

On the other hand, capitalists look to the state for a vast array of supports: laws against labor unions, bailouts in crises, industrial subsidies, global military operations, supportive school curricula, etc. Tensions beset capitalism as some strengthen the state to get more supports for capitalism while others weaken it for fear of what a strong state might do. Thus, the anti-tax party of Trump/GOP imposes tariffs (a tax), launches trade wars, etc. while also encumbering the state with rising budget deficits: strengthening and weakening the state simultaneously.

For a transition to socialism to get underway requires a different politics. A new and genuinely different political party, for example, could offer clear and explicit opposition to capitalism's continuance. It could advocate a systemic alternative (say democratic worker co-ops instead of hierarchical employer/employee capitalism). Politics in the US would then finally emerge from the narrow where two parties agreed on sustaining capitalism only fight over how best to do that. There would finally be a real opposition and real political debate about which alternative system best serves the people's needs.

The development and growth of such a party would change US politics and its relationship to US capitalism. Rs and Ds do all they can, separately and together, to prevent such a party emerging: no surprise there. The question is why the many who grasp the need to get beyond capitalism yet still hesitate about such a party.

This article was published in Common Dreams on August 19, 2018.

Neither Democrats nor Republicans Will Admit the Problem Is Capitalism Itself

September 30, 2019
Truthout

Leaders around the world increasingly worry about the next capitalist recession (or economic downturn) now looming globally. In Europe's strongest economy, Germany, a recession has already arrived in all but formal naming. U.S. manufacturing has declined for the last two quarters. Negative interest rates (where lenders pay borrowers to safely make a loan) are an increasingly widespread sign. Another sign is that lenders charge higher interest rates for short-term vs. long-term loans because they fear an impending recession will make borrowers' ability to repay riskier in the short term. Anxieties about safety reflect the sense of an impending economic crash.

Trump is perhaps the most worried among world leaders fearing recession. Having made the economy a central issue for his re-election effort, he needs the U.S. economy to be in "great" shape. He repeats the few statistics available to support such claims. Yet Trump's fears of a looming recession and its possible consequences for his 2020 re-election are also evident. He recently branded the man he made chair of the U.S. central bank, Jerome Powell, an "enemy" like the leader of China. Powell's refusal to cut interest rates drastically — a classic tool to slow or postpone a recession — was Trump's target. Trump recognizes, as other leaders do, that their political futures hinge on the next recession: on when it hits, how bad it gets, and how long it lasts. Recessions have always haunted the leaders of countries where capitalism is the prevailing system.

The basic cause of current and past downturns in capitalist economies is the system itself. It has been plagued by and subjected its people to the plague of cyclically recurring economic downturns for the last 250 years. They happen on average every four to seven years, although particular conditions of time and place can occasionally make the period longer or shorter. They happen wherever in the world the capitalist system came to prevail. As that prevalence became global, so too have the cyclical downturns.

Profit-driven market capitalism has mechanisms and incentives that generate growth but also repeatedly produce imbalances in the supplies and demands for inputs and outputs. Those imbalances cause price movements that eventually and adversely affect profits. Capitalists then cut back their investments resulting in the unemployment and reduced production that comprise and define recessions and downturns. The downturns offset the initial imbalances enabling capitalism's cycle to repeat.

The recessions are thus not instances of market failures nor instances when markets function imperfectly because of government interventions. Rather, recessions and downturns are how market capitalism "corrects" the imbalances it also causes. In other words, market capitalism has mechanisms of self-healing alongside the mechanisms that make it sick. Those who live in capitalist systems repeatedly suffer through both mechanisms so long as that system prevails.

Capitalism's downturns hurt political leaders' careers because of their effects on the well-being of the masses of people. Widespread losses of jobs and businesses mean many mortgages go unpaid and homes get foreclosed. Parents cannot pay for children to finish higher education. People forego needed medical care leading to later, more costly treatment. Stresses from lost jobs and incomes strain family relations often to breaking points. As all levels of government suffer reduced tax revenues, budget deficits and public debts rise and public services decline just when they are needed more than ever because of the economic downturn. Popular dissatisfaction at downturns and all their effects usually spills over to dissatisfaction with politicians and parties in power when they occur.

Capitalist downturns also provoke thoughtful victims and observers to ask two questions: Why does it happen and what might be done to stop it from happening? Will those questions extend to asking why this system reproduces such downturns so recurringly throughout its history everywhere? Will the process of answering include a discussion of the systemic nature and causes of downturns? Will capitalism itself then become a target for criticism? Might that lead to the really big question lurking in such criticism: Can we do better than capitalism with a system that does not have or need recurring downturns?

Most political leaders of countries where capitalism is the prevailing system know, consciously or not, that their job descriptions include a commandment: Thou shalt not challenge or even question capitalism as a system. Instinctively, self-preservation drives them to find and focus public attention elsewhere. Plausible other, nonsystemic causes need to be defined and denounced. If needed, suitable scapegoats – notably those that have proved useful in the past – need to be blamed. Thus, Trump focuses attacks on the Federal Reserve as the short-run scapegoat (its failure to drop interest rates as far and fast as Trump wants will "cause" recession). Likewise, he attacks Democrats and mass media for exaggerating recession risks purposely to bring the recession that will undermine Trump's re-election.

Similarly, Boris Johnson in the U.K. blames the recession looming there on the European Union (EU), on a delayed Brexit from the EU, on immigrants, and the other usual targets and scapegoats for his Conservative Party. Likewise, many other European leaders follow suit, blaming existing or looming recessions on immigration, on U.S.-China economic warfare, on Brexit, and so on. Much the same leadership patterns appear elsewhere.

It is important to notice how leaders carefully, consistently avoid any critique of the capitalist system and its internal structure for generating yet another economic downturn in its long, long history of doing that repeatedly. That absence speaks very loudly once you note it. The lack of a systemic critique soon becomes routinized. The public is, in effect, trained to see only the external, conjunctural conditions of, and influences, on economic downturns. The taboo applied generally to systemic critique in capitalism then covers the public discussion of capitalism's regular, socially disruptive and immensely costly systemic instability.

Instead of systemic critique, we often get overheated debates over alternative policies to limit, contain and moderate recessions. Conservatives generally have wanted to limit government countercyclical intervention in the economy. They favor minimalism and monetary actions (changing interest rates, quantity of money in circulation). Liberals and social democrats favor larger government interventions with a focus more on fiscal policy (changing taxes and government spending). Thus today, Trump hammers the Fed to get lower interest rates but waffles on a large infrastructure spending program that Democrats prefer, for example.

Far less important than the details of these debates is their shared function. Both sides keep the public from discussing the systemic causes of recurring downturns. Both sides avoid any discussion of systemic change as a logical part of a rational response to the latest or impending downturn. However nuanced or mathematicized the professional economics literature on countercyclical policies, like the popular discourses, it too, keeps system change off the agenda for discussion, let alone policy analyses or prescriptions.

Rarely, a few debaters defensively acknowledge that systemic causes and changes might belong logically in the discussion of capitalist downturns. But doing so, they assure their audiences, would be simply "unrealistic." That is because monetary and fiscal policies fall within what politicians can do, while system change does not. In short, "realism" is their defense for the limitations they place on their studies of and responses to capitalist downturns. But that defense fails. Why and how is it "realistic" to limit public and professional debate and discussion to policies that never end or stop the problem they purport to address?

In the U.S., every president since at least Franklin D. Roosevelt promised the American people that he would not only end the capitalist downturn his administration faced, but also that his policies would make sure such downturns would not afflict succeeding generations. No president could or did keep that promise.

Current Democratic candidates for president, including Elizabeth Warren and Bernie Sanders on the left, have not yet gone beyond the combination of fiscal and monetary anti-recessionary policies captured under the phrase "New Deal." While proposals for a Green New Deal address environmental as well as anti-recessionary needs, they once again hesitate to go beyond them to propose basic system change.

Genuine "realism" would admit those policies' failures and open the public and professional discussion of capitalism's recurring recessions to systemic critiques and solutions involving systemic change.

This article was published in Truthout on September 30, 2019.

Capitalism's Political Servants: Trump and Johnson

February 11, 2020
CounterPunch

For the last half-century, US and UK capitalisms led the way in undoing the parallel legacies of the New Deal and Europe's social democracies. From its ascending Thatcher-Reagan couple to its descending Trump-Johnson imitation, neoliberal capitalism replaced Keynesian capitalism. Private corporate capitalists funded effective campaigns to celebrate neo-liberalism. The US and UK institutionalized it by de-regulating and privatizing further and faster than anywhere else.

Over the same period, private capitalists attacked the working class on three fronts. Neo-liberalism provided ideological cover in that attack. Its ideologues insisted that their goals — deregulation and privatization — would bring prosperity and growth to all, a win-win program for everyone. Neoliberalism swept up many Keynesians and social democrats. They had wavered especially after the 1960s when they could no longer preserve, let alone advance, working-class gains won in the post-1929 depression. Resigned to neoliberalism, many leaders of center-left, labor and socialist parties redefined themselves as merely advocates for its less harsh forms.

The first front in capitalism's attack was outsourcing production and jobs. At first, manufacturing moved from capitalism's old centers (western Europe, US, Japan) to China, India, and other low-wage areas. Large profits gained by early outsourcers forced much competitive outsourcing later. Many service industries followed. Neo-liberals hailed "globalization." To them it showed efficiency and prosperity delivered by deregulation and privatization.

Less movable employers (construction, retail trade, fast-food, etc.) raised profits by opening a second front against the working class. They chose increasingly to hire low wage immigrants desperate to escape from economic, political and military crises in their home countries. The undocumented were especially attractive: they lacked legal recourse for unpaid wages, illegal job conditions, etc. Their labor was unprotected.

The third front in the employers' attack was more important than outsourcing or immigration. In a new automation wave, computers, robots, and artificial intelligence boosted profits by displacing workers. Automation enabled employers to cut wage bills relative to revenues from sales. Ideologues then attributed rising profits to neo-liberal capitalism's win-win globalization.

Neo-liberal ideology did not last long. Widening gaps between winners and losers from globalization strengthened ideological critiques of win-win claims. Corporations, stock markets, venture capitalists, and the few they enriched (capital gains, dividends, merger fees, etc.) were clear winners. Top executives scored huge pay packages. Top "professional advisors" enjoyed big salaries and bonuses. Losers, on the other hand, were almost everyone else, a vast majority. Workers suffered stagnant wages and deteriorating jobs. Large industrial cities (Detroit, Cleveland, etc.) atrophied alongside small "rust belt" cities and much of rural America.

Average real wages stagnated since the 1970s. Chasing the "American Dream" drove millions to incur mounting personal debts (mortgage, auto loans, credit cards and then student loans). That added credit anxieties to their accumulating anguish over flat real wages, eroding benefits, and ever less job security. Capital's three-pronged attack hurt.

Exporting jobs, importing low-wage immigrants, and automation combined to generate that great-for-capitalism mix of rising productivity and stagnant wages. Starting in the 1980s, profits soared and lifted stock markets. Those profits provided much of the money they loaned to a working class borrowing to offset stagnant wages. Rising personal debts proved a fragile economic foundation although they helped obscure the fast-growing rich-poor gap.

The 2008 crash rendered painfully visible what had been obscured. It broke the promises from politicians, academics and the media that lessons learned and reforms installed guaranteed that 1929-type crashes would never recur. The 2008 crash also exposed harsh social realities. The US and UK had become sharply more unequal economically and politically. Both governments quickly endorsed very expensive bailouts for the same banks that had helped cause the crash. Both governments paid for bailouts with decreasingly progressive tax revenues and still more borrowing. And both then pointed to rising government debt to justify austerity for everyone else. The only difference: Labor and the Democrats advocated a less harsh austerity than Conservatives and the Republicans.

Once exposed as performing so much better for the employer class than for the employee class, capitalisms run big risks. Systemic questions and criticisms arise, challenge the status quo, and strengthen social movements for systemic change. That happened during past capitalist crashes and certainly after 1929. Capitalism needs system-preserving political and ideological programs to "get through" crashes even more than it needs them between crashes.

Since 2008 nationalism once again played a key role in capitalism's self-preservation. It had done so earlier in, for example, Mussolini's and Hitler's promises to make Italy and Germany "great again" against enemies – mostly foreign but also domestic (those not "genuinely" Italian or Aryan). Nationalist (in the sense of anti-foreign) ideology covered the state-managed (i.e., fascist) reinforcement or reconstruction of the employer-employee relationship that defines capitalism and that had been sharply challenged in and by the 1930s depression. Trump's "Make America great again" plays to many Americans' sense of loss before and after 2008. He attacks immigrants and "cheating" foreign trade partners as if they caused Americans' felt losses. In the UK, Johnson's Brexit program excoriates "Europeans," as if they caused the UK's deep economic and political inequalities. Bashing and limiting foreigners including immigrants are main themes of capitalism's current political servants.

Those servants protect capitalism from its own crashes and from its highly unequal and very unpopular policy responses. They often choose nationalism because it serves them well. There is nothing new in that.

The left needs to respond in three key ways. First, it should stress how world war and holocaust resulted the last time post-crash capitalism used nationalism for scapegoating. Second, it should expose scapegoat politics as aimed to deflect working class anger from a crash-prone capitalism. Immigration, trade, tariff policies, or European integration define capitalism's preferred terrain of debate, not a critical left's. The left's core response to capitalist nationalism should be this: capitalism is the problem and transition to a new, different, and fundamentally democratic system is the answer.

That answer focuses on the democratization of enterprises. Reforms of capitalism (welfare systems, New Deals, social democracies, etc.), however valuable and hard fought, are never secure while production is organized capitalistically. A small minority then owns and operates enterprises (public and/or private), reaps the profits, and rules each enterprise's majority, its employees. It then uses those profits and that power to undo whatever reforms the working class has won.

The de-facto monarchy/oligarchy inside capitalist enterprises contradicts democracy today as utterly as monarchy and oligarchy outside enterprises did historically. Because reforms of kingdoms rarely endured, modern society eventually abolished monarchies. Reforms of capitalist enterprises likewise rarely endure. What we need are worker coops to democratize enterprises by displacing their capitalists.

40

Capitalism's political servants, past and present, reformists and neoliberals, private boards of directors and public state managers, reproduce that system. After the 2008 crash, bailouts, austerity, and widening inequality, capitalism and its political servants are now especially vulnerable. System change is this historical moment's opportunity. It should be our political project.

This article was published in CounterPunch on February 11, 2020.

The Stimulus Package – Too Little, Too Late

March 19 & 26, 2020
Thom Hartmann Program

The Coronavirus Aid, Relief, and Economic Security (CARES) Act is, for me, a spectacular disappointment. It's too little, too late. It does not recognize the systemic roots of this problem. It's going to throw more money, a lot more money, at the economy, not learning that this didn't solve our problem back in 2008-2009. Doing the same thing now, while cutting interest rates to next to nothing, risks leading this economic system to go on a binge of borrowing that the world has never seen before.

For the last decade, we've been on the life support of a debt-ridden system on a scale no professional economist could have even imagined. What we are doing now is again the same thing. "Free money, every business! Come, borrow! Get yourself through this disaster!" Economically, we're not changing anything fundamental. We're not learning the lessons of the obvious failure to plan properly to handle a viral pandemic, even though we've had a dozen of them in the last century, some of which were very deadly.

I see a society, to be honest, sticking its head in the sand for fear of recognizing that this society needs fundamental economic changes and it has for a long time. We're about to go through yet another crisis, not having learned the lesson, repeating the mistakes of the past, which will set up the next crisis. It's very disheartening.

We have to understand that an economic system is judged by how well it organizes the community it is supposed to serve. Virtually everyone understands that extreme inequality has enormously socially disruptive effects. I know that there are some of my friends who want to blame Mr. Trump for the divisiveness that rocks this country, and sure he deserves lots of blame. But to only blame him, is to miss the point again.

We have redistributed upward the wealth and income in our country over the last 40 years, away from the poor and middle class to a small group at the top. Nothing in the stimulus plan that is being discussed by the House and Senate addresses that fundamental flaw in our system. Therefore, it does not deal with many of the root causes of what brought us to (1) the crisis of 2008, (2) the last 10 years of an economy on life support-levels of debt, and (3) the lack of preparedness over that time to develop a society capable of handling a serious viral outbreak. Our government, abetted by the media, doesn't want to look at any of it.

Even the Chinese (who call themselves socialists) and the South Koreans (who call themselves capitalists) were able to mobilize both public and private resources to fight back against this virus, and they've done a very good job. We could do the same. Americans have every capacity that these other countries do, if not more. But our system precluded, prevented, undermined, and slowed taking parallel steps.

The $2 trillion that the government now proposes to spend will be paid for, in large part, by government debt and it will encourage our corporate sector, already laden with record levels of debt, to borrow even more. The amount of money thrown to average people of a $1,200 check (which many won't even get) is crumbs off the table. It is an insult both to our intelligence and to the scope of the problem we face.

The other lesson that we should have learned is that, if you don't fundamentally change the system, as fast as you can make a reform, the interests gripped by those reforms will do everything in their power to undo them. A gross example is the 1933 Banking Act, otherwise known as the Glass-Steagall Act. The banks didn't want it. They fought it. When they lost that battle and it got passed, they went to work to undo it. Over the intervening years, first they evaded it, then they weakened it, and under the presidency of Bill Clinton they finally had it repealed. I mention this repeal by Bill Clinton because the Democrats are as responsible as the Republicans of working against the interests of the majority of Americans. Clinton's repeal was an example of reform being undone: reforms just don't go far enough.

Yet today, all we see is more reforms. You may have noticed that the stimulus started as a few billion dollars, but was soon increased to trillions of dollars worth of aid. That gives you a scale of our so-called leaders' lack of control.

The reality is that they don't know what to do beyond reforms. That's not because they aren't smart; they are hampered by a system which focuses their attention and causes their acts to work in such a way that has led to the total mess we're in now.

I've tried to argue over the last 10 to 12 years that we've had to learn the lesson of 2008. I assume I'll continue to do much the same now. You can trickle down, which is what we're doing again, or you could trickle up, which would be to help the people at the bottom. That would put the burden of adjustment on the corporate and business sector, and would likely garner support from the mass of people. At the very least, even if it didn't work, you'd have helped the majority. Instead, our leaders help the minority at the top. For a country that calls itself democratic, this is a bizarre way to undertake economic policy.

This essay has been adapted from two appearances of Professor Wolff's on the Thom Hartmann Program, on March 19 and March 26, 2020.

Sticking Your Head in the Sand: The Stimulus Bill & Mortgage Securities

April 2, 2020
Loud & Clear with Brian Becker

The March 2020 Coronavirus Aid, Relief, and Economic Security Act (CARES Act) will be remembered for a long time as a remarkable exercise in sticking your head into the sand. Everything about this bill is an attempt to look upon the current crisis as a temporary, short-term blip that needs to be addressed so that we can get back to where we were before the virus hit. The fundamental flaw of this program is that it fails to understand two things: (1) that the economic condition of the United States and the world before the virus was not good; it was terrible, and (2) that the bad conditions of that economic system were precisely major contributors to what we are experiencing now. To say the same thing in another way, our current economic collapse is not attributable 100 percent, or anything like that, to the virus. It is at least equally a reflection of fundamental weaknesses, flaws, and structural imbalances in the capitalist economy.

So far, nobody in either the Republican Party or the Democratic Party has been able to point a finger at the capitalist system we live in and to pinpoint the severe weaknesses that make it vulnerable in the way exposed by this virus. They are not asking the difficult questions. In their minds they have to spend trillions of dollars because if they don't, the game is over. So, they're not interested in the details. They don't give a damn whether they help an industry that doesn't need it. That's all window dressing for the evening news. They are desperate.

Currently, not a lot of money is moving around in the system because everybody's hunkered down, nobody is getting an income the way they did, and nobody is spending money the way they did. All kinds of businesses are not earning money, and all kinds of banks are not being paid for the mortgages they issued. People either think, or hope, they don't have to continue payment, or they simply don't have the money to do so.

So, the government got nervous that there would now be a housing crisis. The Fed then bought more mortgage-backed securities in the hopes that it would leave banks feeling good about issuing more mortgages to keep the housing economy going. Because if banks don't issue mortgages, nobody can buy a house. And if you can't buy a house, the people trying to sell a house can't sell it. And that creates more economic stress.

What the government hadn't counted on, because there's no planning, is that all kinds of dealers in mortgage-backed securities were terrified that the current crisis might lead to a rise in mortgage rates. Credit markets expected banks around the country to say that it's dangerous to give people money to buy a house because whatever income they had they may not have in the next several months. So, banks had been buying a kind of insurance to protect them against interest rates for housing going up. But because of the Fed's decision to buy all those mortgage-backed securities, rates did the opposite.

They drove interest rates down, but they still did not give any incentive for people to go borrow because of the crazy situation we're in. Nobody who's contemplating buying a house is going to go through with it now. It's too dangerous to get yourself loaded up with a 20- or 30-year mortgage.

So, the disconnect between what people are doing in the way of buying homes and what the banks would do in this crazy time led the Fed to drive down interest rates after banks had purchased very expensive insurance against the opposite. This means that the banks and others who deal in mortgage-backed securities are now stuck. They spent a lot of money on insurance they didn't need and they don't have the money now to carry on their normal business.

They've begged the Federal Reserve to undo today what it did yesterday. That is a crazy level of disorganization and chaos. You can count on President Trump to act, if he's asked about this, not as though he understands it, but to act as if it's all under control. But nothing is under control. This is uncharted territory, and the chaos in the mortgage market is just a symptom of what you're going to be seeing. Half of it will be hidden from us and will explode into the headlines the way the mortgage crisis just did.

It's too early to say what the outcome of all this will be, but we don't have to speculate about whether or not people will be defaulting on their mortgages. They already are. The chaos in the mortgage-securities market is all about people who are not paying their mortgages, either because they have no income left with which to pay or because they have to devote their income to the immediate priorities like food and heat. The only question now is what do you do in a system like ours, where you have a collapse of the economy throwing millions of people into a situation where they don't have the money with which to pay for housing?

We're going to be seeing lots of crazy back and forth because government leaders literally don't know what they're doing. We're going to see this kind of chaos driven by the absurdity of trying to re-create the economy before the virus, which is crazy because that economy is as responsible for the collapse now as is the virus itself.

This essay has been adapted from an appearance of Professor Wolff's on the program Loud & Clear with Brian Becker which aired on April 2, 2020.

COVID-19 and the Failures of Capitalism

April 6, 2020
CounterPunch

The desperate policies of panic-driven governments involve throwing huge amounts of money at the economies collapsed in response to the coronavirus threat. Monetary authorities create money and lend it at extremely low interest rates to the major corporations and especially big banks "to get them through the crisis." Government treasuries borrow vast sums to get the collapsed economy back into what they imagine is "the normal, pre-virus economy." Capitalism's leaders are rushing into policy failures because of their ideological blinders.

The problem of policies aimed to return the economy to what it was before the virus hit is this: Global capitalism, by 2019, was itself a major cause of the collapse in 2020. Capitalism's scars from the crashes of 2000 and 2008-2009 had not healed. Years of low interest rates had enabled corporations and governments to "solve" all their problems by borrowing limitlessly at almost zero interest rate cost. All the new money pumped into economies by central banks had indeed caused the feared inflation, but chiefly in stock markets whose prices consequently spiraled dangerously far away from underlying economic values and realities. Inequalities of income and wealth reached historic highs.

In short, capitalism had built up vulnerabilities to another crash that any number of possible triggers could unleash. The trigger this time was not the dot.com meltdown of 2000 or the sub-prime meltdown of 2008/9; it was a virus. And of course, mainstream ideology requires focusing on the trigger, not the vulnerability. Thus, mainstream policies aim to reestablish pre-virus capitalism. Even if they succeed, that will return us to a capitalist system whose accumulated vulnerabilities will soon again collapse from yet another trigger.

In the light of the coronavirus pandemic, I focus criticism on capitalism and the vulnerabilities it has accumulated for several reasons. Viruses are part of nature. They have attacked human beings—sometimes dangerously—in both distant and recent history. In 1918, the Spanish Flu killed nearly 700,000 in the United States and millions elsewhere. Recent viruses include SARS, MERS and Ebola. What matters to public health is each society's preparedness: stockpiled tests, masks, ventilators, hospital beds, trained personnel, etc., to manage dangerous viruses. In the U.S., such objects are produced by private capitalist enterprises whose goal is profit.

It was not profitable to produce and stockpile such products, that was not and still is not being done.

Nor did the U.S. government produce or stockpile those medical products. Top U.S. government personnel privilege private capitalism; it is their primary objective to protect and strengthen. The result is that neither private capitalism nor the U.S. government performed the most basic duty of any economic system: to protect and maintain public health and safety. U.S. capitalism's response to the coronavirus pandemic continues to be what it has been since December 2019: too little, too late. It failed. It is the problem.

The second reason I focus on capitalism is that the responses to today's economic collapse by Trump, the GOP and most Democrats carefully avoid any criticism of capitalism. They all debate the virus, China, foreigners, other politicians, but never the system they all serve. When Trump and others press people to return to churches and jobs—despite risking their and others' lives—they place reviving a collapsed capitalism ahead of public health.

The third reason capitalism gets blame here is that alternative systems— those not driven by a profit-first logic—could manage viruses better. While not profitable to produce and stockpile everything needed for a viral pandemic, it is efficient. The wealth already lost in this pandemic far exceeds the cost to have produced and stockpiled the tests and ventilators, the lack of which is contributing so much to today's disaster. Capitalism often pursues profit at the expense of more urgent social needs and values. In this, capitalism is grossly inefficient. This pandemic is now bringing that truth home to people.

A worker-coop based economy—where workers democratically run enterprises, deciding what, how and where to produce, and what to do with any profits—could, and likely would, put social needs and goals (like proper preparation for pandemics) ahead of profits. Workers are the majority in all capitalist societies; their interests are those of the majority. Employers are always a small minority; theirs are the "special interests" of that minority. Capitalism gives that minority the position, profits and power to determine how the society as a whole lives or dies. That's why all employees now wonder and worry about how long our jobs, incomes, homes and bank accounts will last—if we still have them. A minority (employers) decides all those questions and excludes the majority (employees) from making those decisions, even though that majority must live with their results.

Of course, the top priority now is to put public health and safety first. To that end, employees across the country are now thinking about refusing to obey orders to work in unsafe job conditions. U.S. capitalism has thus placed a general strike on today's social agenda. A close second priority is to learn from capitalism's failure in the face of the pandemic. We must not suffer such a dangerous and unnecessary social breakdown again. Thus, system change is now also moving onto today's social agenda.

This article was published in CounterPunch on April 6, 2020.

Unemployment: Cruel, Wasteful, Unnecessary

May 11, 2020
Economic Update: Unemployment - Cruel, Wasteful, Unnecessary

Today, over 30 million Americans are unemployed according to the official statistics. That is likely an underestimation. We must address this cataclysm of unemployment, because we don't really need it. It is very cruel to the people who suffer it directly, and it is cruel to those who suffer it indirectly when someone close to them becomes and remains unemployed. And the worst of it is that it's a waste of human resources and all the means of production that sit idle when unemployed people do not use them. It's a terrible inefficiency due to our economic system — capitalism.

Unemployment happens when a capitalist, an employer, finds it more profitable to not have a worker than to have one. Employers either do not hire workers in the first place, or they fire those already working. There it is. Unemployment is a decision made by employers.

Unemployment always involves redistributing wealth. You may not have thought of it that way, but let me show you why that's always involved. We begin by remembering what you like when you're not unemployed and you're working. You take things out of the economy — the things you consume — and you put things into the economy — the things you help to produce. You take, you give. When you're unemployed, you continue to take. You don't stop eating, you don't stop drinking, etc. But you do stop working and producing. You take out of the economy, but you don't put back into it, because you're not employed. That means that part of the wealth produced by the people still working has to be redistributed. We redistribute wealth, for example, by taxing some or all employed people and transferring that money to the unemployed so that they can go to the store and buy what they need. And that means the people who are taxed can't spend the money that they pay in taxes. That's how the redistribution gets done. But you also do it in your home. If one of the two members of an adult family is unemployed, they share in the income of the one who still has a job. That's another redistribution that wasn't necessary prior to the first person losing their job.

Unemployment is a cruelty for the unemployed and those around them: just think of the way people feel about themselves when they can't work, when they have to rely either on taxes, on the sharing of a spouse or others, or if they have to use their savings. But here's the double irony: capitalists lose too. If they don't have people working, they're not going to make profits. So, everybody loses from unemployment — the workers who are unemployed, the people still employed who have to help take care of those that are unemployed, and the employer themselves.

So why does unemployment, this unnecessary thing that's bad for everyone, really happen? It's because capitalists have reasons to suffer the losses of unemployment in a way workers don't. There's nothing in it for workers, but there is something in it for the employers.

When times get tough, employers figure they lose less profits by laying off people than if they kept them in their positions. In other words, when the wages paid to workers are more than the profits that capitalist employers get from having workers, the workers lose their jobs because employers take care of business first and foremost. But there's another reason. It's kind of good for capitalism to have unemployment. Yes, it's bad that those workers aren't making profits for some employer somewhere. But all employers know that if workers are always unemployed, it's a tool for discipline. "Don't act up", the capitalists can tell the worker, "because there's lots of unemployed people out there who would be more than willing to have your job." This epitomizes the irrationality of capitalism, the crazy system that needs to keep people unemployed even though nobody wants it, except those who need to keep the upper hand at the workplace.

Here's something much better than unemployment. I'm going to call it re-employment. Imagine if we didn't allow unemployment and the minute a private employer didn't hire you or fired you, you would be immediately re-employed. You'd be put back to work and never be unemployed. We would outlaw unemployment like we outlawed slavery, peonage, debt prisons, and all the other horrible things we've gotten rid of over the centuries. There'd be no need to redistribute wealth or to fight over how we do that, to fight over taxes, to fight over sharing scarce output. We wouldn't have that problem. We wouldn't need to redistribute wealth, because the system wouldn't deprive anyone of a job. We wouldn't have all the cruel suffering for people who undergo unemployment. We would not be paying benefits — that is what the money we give unemployed people — without getting something back from them, which is something that has irked many of you and for good reason.

Here's another irony. We've already done something like that. We did that in the Great Depression of the 1930s. Between 1934 and 1941, the key years of the Great Depression, the federal government said to workers who were fired by their private employers, "We, the government, will put you back to work. We will re-employ you." The government became what we call "the employer of last resort". If the private sector either could not or would not give people a job, if the private employers choose to fire their workers, the government hired them. Millions of workers in the 1930s — we estimate about 15 million — did not have to rely on benefits from the government, from their relatives, or from the church to survive. We didn't need to pay unemployment benefits, because people weren't unemployed, but re-employed by the government. By receiving a salary as opposed to unemployment benefits, those people worked and thereby gave back to society.

Let me offer two brief examples. One was called the WPA, the Works Progress Administration. This was for artists. What an interesting idea: to all the people who lost their job as singers, dancers, painters, sculptors, craftspeople of one kind or another, the government said, "Come. We'll hire you." They hired them and created teams of actors, poets, writers, and they moved them around the United States to provide lessons and performances across the country. It was the greatest cultural production in American history. People who had never had a theater troupe in their community, had one. People who had never taught young people in the community, could. It was spectacular.

The Civilian Conservation Corps was the other government program for which people were hired. Its members were the first to do ecological and environmental projects across America. They reforested the land. They cleared swamps and rerouted rivers. They built the national parks in the Western part of our country that many of us enjoy. There were other examples of useful projects produced by people who were paid salaries. What a wonderfully better way of doing things than letting people languish on unemployment.

People sometimes ask me, "Why is it not a known fact that we had federal jobs during the Great Depression?" The reason has to do with our education system. I was struck in the early days and months of the Obama administration that we didn't have a federal jobs program then. Why did Democrats have an amnesia attack and forget about the last time we were in a crisis similar to the one of 2008-2009? There was no discussion then about a federal jobs program, and there isn't one now even though there ought to be. Otherwise, we're not only not learning from history, we're condemning ourselves to an unemployment that is unnecessary, wasteful, and deeply inefficient.

What the U.S. didn't do in the Great Depression is also important. They could have re-employed the unemployed by establishing worker co-ops, saying to unemployed people, "Here, we're going to give you the funds and the system. Set up your own collective co-op business." By doing that, not only would they have given back to society, but they would have created a new way of doing business, a collective, democratic, community-based way of doing things. It could have built a whole cooperative sector of the American economy that would allow all Americans to compare what's that like and maybe understand that it would be better than the capitalist, hierarchical, top–down system. We would have learned a new way to produce, organize, and build democracy starting from the workplace, where it's long overdue.

Today, we could have a program that combines jobs created by the federal government and worker co-ops in which the federal government provides the support, the encouragement, the funds, and then writes contracts with such worker co-ops to produce goods and services for the United States to consume. We could even give unemployed people a choice between unemployment and re-employment, and build in the incentives toward the most socially desirable choice (the latter): what you earn in a worker co-op or federal job would be more than what you get from simply sitting unemployed.

What could the re-employment be used for? What could unemployed people give back to society if they were given the opportunity? First, a national mass testing program, which has become necessary for the last two months at least. We could use thousands, millions even, of the unemployed to do this kind of testing quickly. At the time this episode was recorded, less than 2% of Americans had been tested for COVID-19. The unemployed people who are not infected should be known and identified so that they can be trained to be testers. The not-infected are the ones who should be sent back to work the soonest, because they endanger neither the public they interact with nor one another. Subsequent testing would have to be done continuously, something a few people seem to not understand. Asymptomatic people are not as safe as those who test negative, but are nevertheless less likely to spread the disease because they don't for instance cough as frequently as symptomatic individuals. The latter are the ones that need help with treatment and quarantine periods.

A national mass testing program would keep us safe and allow us to return to work, something many want, in a safe way. Not setting up a mass testing program thanks to the labor of the currently unemployed is unnecessary, wasteful, and deeply inefficient. We shouldn't let a capitalist system deprive us this way. The unemployed want a job. We need the testing. And this capitalist system can't put two and two together.

Second, we could use unemployed people to do what private capitalists didn't do. The unemployed could produce, stockpile, and monitor test kits, masks, gloves, ventilators, beds, hospitals, ICUs. In other words, we can be prepared for the next wave of this coronavirus or any other virus or pandemic that comes. We can have the preparation, using the unemployed, to make sure that doesn't happen again. That will give unemployed people very meaningful work that is very socially useful and that we badly need.

We also have to reorganize all the factories, the offices, and the stores, so that they are safe. That means reconfiguring where all the machines, the desks, and the counters are so that we can remain far apart enough to be safe. We also need a new commitment to cleaning and disinfecting on an ongoing basis. There need to be people trained in how best to do that with the least disruption to the life of a factory, of an office, or of a store. The unemployed could be made to be those trained people.

All of these unemployed teachers from kindergarten through college could be organized to do tutoring. Millions of people need to learn and be educated, both school children and adults. Let's have a real continuing education mentality. Let the people who are unemployed, who have skills — all kinds of skills — begin to teach others. We have the digital capacity that can allow us to do it, it just needs to be organized.

We also have a climate change crisis. You don't hear about it so much right now because the virus has controlled the headlines. But we are desperately in need of dealing with climate change. Unemployed people could be reforesting parts of America. Planting trees is something that can be done with social distancing. Plus, we'd know from the testing who's not infected, who doesn't have the problem, who can be put on the front line. We need to build parks. We need to recapture the carbon that goes into the atmosphere and causes temperature increases. We need to reduce carbon emissions. We need a mass public transportation system so that we rely less on the private automobile, which is the single largest source of air pollution in our society.

There's lots of work to do. We need to rehire the unemployed, who can and want to give back to society, to do a lot of it. However, unemployment and unemployment compensation are inventions of capitalism. Capitalism needs to fire people when it's profitable. And it needs to have a "reserve army of the unemployed" so that all workers are well-disciplined. So, don't be fooled. Even though unemployment is bad for capitalism in so far as it erodes profits, it is good for the system as it helps capitalists stay on top. For the worker, though, unemployment is unilaterally bad. But they get no choice, because the system has decided for them. Capitalism would rather suffer the loss of unemployment than suffer the risk of a workforce unafraid to demand adequate wage conditions, safe workplaces, a decent work-life balance, etc.

We are living through a collapse of capitalism in the face of a virus and in the face of its own unfortunate tendency to think that unemployment is a reasonable thing for society. It never was and it isn't now. What it always has been, is a cataclysmic waste. As stated, we can do better than unemployment. What I've tried to do is give you as concrete a way as possible of seeing that the much better alternative of re-employment would allow us to not only give people the dignity of a job, but also to create a tangible, sizeable worker co-op sector of the American economy in every community. Let the people decide what kind of a mix of worker co-op and capitalist enterprises they want.

Our dominant capitalist system failed to prepare for this virus because it wasn't profitable to produce the tests, the masks, the gloves, etc. Our government, believing that private enterprises are the end-all-be-all, didn't make up for their failures. Our political leaders are the creatures of capitalism just as much as the CEOs of any given company are. Politicians doubled down on the market failure by allowing 30 million people to be thrown out of work during an epidemiological emergency. We should have and could have prepared for this, and we should never have followed up the health crisis with an economic one. But now we're going through another crash, and we have people cooped up at home without a job, a harmful imposition that in other circumstances would not have been necessary. Re-employment would not only be better than unemployment, but it would also teach us what it means in practical terms to do better than capitalism. Staying with capitalism now is wasteful and unnecessary too. We *can* do better.

This essay has been adapted from "Economic Update: Unemployment - Cruel, Wasteful, Unnecessary" which was published on Democracy at Work's YouTube channel on May 11, 2020.

Mass Unemployment is a Policy Choice

May 26, 2020
Loud & Clear with Brian Becker

We are now in a depression, not a downturn or economic bump. Having more or less 30 million unemployed people, no one knows for sure, is characteristic of a depression. Moreover, no one knows what's going to happen come election time. Predicting the future is like going to a carnival and taking the fortune teller seriously, rather than as an amusement.

The story being told by the folks in Congress about what's going on in this country is a desperate use of advertising to cover a reality that is very different. True patriotism is the ability to face problems and recognize the faults in the system in order to overcome them. Celebrating America as the "greatest" economy in the world, these days, is nothing more than false advertising.

Our politicians are very distant from the average person. They are mostly wealthy, white men. Demonstrating this disconnect, White House economic adviser, Kevin Hassett, recently referred to workers as "human capital stock." This is a way to treat human beings as if they were interchangeable with other parts of the production process: tools, equipment, buildings, raw materials, and other inanimate objects. Capitalism makes it too painful for employers to recognize that employees are human beings. Firing thirty million of them means you are really hurting them, their spouses, their children, their elderly who depend on them, their friends, their neighbors, and their relatives. It is easier, perhaps, to think of workers as pieces of furniture or machines—as capital. But, when employers dump people into months of unemployment while forcing them to stay inside and worry about the dangers of the coronavirus, it becomes catastrophic for all. Physical and mental health deteriorate; and you end up deteriorating your "human capital stock" by pretending that it's still standing there like a machine waiting to be turned on again. Such a misunderstanding of the human experience is another one of capitalism's heavy costs.

Our current mass unemployment was barely opposed, even by the Democratic Party. A party which only quibbled with minor details of this reality. They wanted to be a bit more generous with little checks given to people, and made some improvements in unemployment compensation. But, basically neither the labor movement, nor the Democrats in government organized a massive opposition. Massive unemployment was indeed a policy choice by both major parties.

The truth is that unemployment in neoclassical economics is a mechanism for disciplining the working class. It's preferred by capitalists. Full employment has always been a term that conservatives and liberals have argued about. In 1946, a bill was passed that was originally called the Full Employment Act. Eventually it was called the Employment Act. The name was changed during the negotiations in Congress. With President Roosevelt deceased, Congress began to whittle down the power of the New Deal. They didn't want the government to ensure full employment. So, the wording in the final bill was changed to Maximum Employment. But of course, the word "maximum" is vague. It is simply a loophole that allows for a certain amount of people to always be ready to be hired if a business wants them. The idea is that such a reserve army of unemployed workers will be desperately eager for a job; this way, employers can get them without having to raise their wages.

The theory of the "reserve army of the unemployed" has been around for 200 years. It means that capitalism always maintains some form of unemployment because it's convenient to employers. If everybody is working, a business that wants to grow and hire more workers will have to look for them in another place, where they're already working. To convince an employed worker to come work for you instead requires them to offer higher wages. Employers don't want to be in that position. They'd like to have the convenience of having a perpetual pool of unemployed workers.

A reserve army of the unemployed does benefit employers in another way. Employed workers know: if you don't accept what the employer dishes out, those unemployed people out there will take your job. Unemployed workers scare employed workers into being docile.

The only time the United States ever got close to full employment—by which I mean one percent or less of the labor force out of work—was during World War II. In that case, we put half of the unemployed into uniforms and the other half into making the uniforms and other military materials. We could give the unemployed useful jobs at any time, but it's only been in warfare when the country's survival is at stake that capitalists allow the temporary disappearance of the reserve army of the unemployed.

Today, we face the coronavirus pandemic and an economic depression. There are a variety of ways this can play out. One of them is that the economy bounces back quickly in the same two months or so that it took to hit it so far down. Another scenario is that it will take a good six months to a year for things to return to normal. Others believe it can take a decade or more; and then there are those who believe it will never come back.

There are good arguments for why those are the scenarios. The bottom line is that we don't know what the future holds.

What is clear, however, is that President Trump is scared to death that he will be in a re-election campaign at a time when people are overwhelmed, or nearly so, by a virus that his government did not prepare for, did not know how to deal with, waited too long, and then did too little to address. That's going to haunt him, and it's going to hurt him. On top of that, to have the second worst, or quite possibly the worst crash in US capitalist history, he can potentially kiss his re-election goodbye. As a result, he is doing everything he can to reduce these two obstacles to re-election. He reduces the problem of the virus by pretending he's got it under control when he clearly doesn't. He pretends there's testing going on when we know for sure that we haven't tested, but five percent of our population. And he doesn't wear a mask in public to minimize and downplay the threat of the virus.

The same goes for the economy. He wants to "reopen the economy." That is a thin argument for basically saying he has to get people back to work because they're going to blame him for the extreme levels of unemployment. So, here he is pushing, ordering, pressuring people who are desperate to return to a workplace, which in many cases or perhaps in most cases, has not been made anywhere near adequately safe to return to. It is a very dangerous gamble by a very desperate politician.

In our current crisis, the recently passed The Coronavirus Aid, Relief, and Economic Security Act (the CARES Act) is a program invented by and for capitalists; it provides employers with money and it affords them the discretion of how to use it. Of course, they will use it to make profits for their company. Capitalists will lower wages and benefits, and if the workers don't like it, they will simply hire some of the reserve army of unemployed workers. The still employed, who are currently glad to escape unemployment, will soon be hit with the consequences of mass unemployment: employers are even further empowered over their workers. That's what was accomplished here by a policy decision.

This program (CARES) is supposed to fix a broken economy but gives the people at the top even more money and even more leeway to use it in the same ways that brought us into this crisis in the first place. What is clear more than ever are the desperate levels of self-delusion and denial of the capitalist class.

This essay has been adapted from an appearance of Professor Wolff's on the program Loud & Clear with Brian Becker which aired on May 26, 2020.

Why the Neoliberal Agenda Is a Failure at Fighting Coronavirus

May 29, 2020
Independent Media Institute

The utter failure of private capitalism to prepare for the coronavirus should have surprised no one. Private capitalism, as business school graduates repeat, focuses on profit. The "profit incentive," they learn, makes private capitalism the superior, "most efficient" economic system available. That is its "bottom line" and "chief goal." The problem is that to produce adequate numbers of testing components, masks, gloves, ventilators, hospital beds, etc., and then to store, secure, monitor, maintain and demographically stockpile them were not and are not privately profitable businesses.

A private capitalist producer of those goods would have to wait, perhaps a long time, for them to become marketable. The risk is great, the future price unknowable, and profitability hard to count on. So private capitalists looked and found elsewhere to invest. They did not produce or stockpile the items needed to secure the public's health by preventing or minimizing a viral pandemic.

Of course, private capitalism's failures could have been offset if governments compensated for them. Governments might have purchased the necessary medical supplies from private capitalists as they emerged from production at prices yielding them good profits. Governments could then have stored, monitored, replenished, and stockpiled them, and absorbed the costs and risks involved. Indeed, governments in many countries did that. But few maintained stockpiles sufficient for "abnormal" or "serious" viral threats. Most stockpiled only smaller "normal flu" levels of the needed medical supplies.

Ideas and practices of government compensating for private capitalism's failures and flaws are old. Business cycle downturns have brought repeated government economic interventions. They do so now. Another pertinent example is government intervention to procure military supplies. It is privately unprofitable to produce, store, secure, monitor, and strategically stockpile tanks, missiles, guns, airplanes, etc., needed for war or "defense." Private capitalists would not likely produce or import them given the risks and uncertainties of future military conflict. So, governments contract to buy them as they are produced at prices profitable for private producers of military supplies. Governments cover the costs and risks of storing, securing, and stockpiling. These immense government subsidies to private capitalists get justified as requirements of national security.

What governments do to prepare for military security they do not do (or do inadequately) for health security from, for example, dangerous microbes. Yet viruses have threatened human beings at least as long as military conflict has. Many more Americans were killed by the 1918 influenza pandemic than died in the 1914-1918 world war. Coronavirus has already killed many more Americans than died in the Vietnam War.

Why then do governments compensate for private capitalism's failures in the military but compensate so much less in the medical industries? And when governments do compensate in the latter, why so differently, varying from much in some countries to little to almost nothing in others?

Neoliberalism's ideological power, varying from country to country, provides an answer. Where it is strong, governments minimize economic interventions. They cultivate blindness to private capitalism's failures and often simply deny them. Officials thus cannot publicly and explicitly undertake to "compensate for failures" in, say, the private medical industries. Trump expressed his neoliberalism by dissolving Obama's White House pandemic preparedness organization.

Neoliberalism argues for laissez-faire. Private enterprises left alone to produce and market without governmental taxation, regulation, etc., will outperform systems where governments intervene. Neoliberalism celebrates the private over the governmental nearly everywhere. It is a kind of fundamentalism in economics: God is private, while the devil is government. The exceptions—the military, police, and judiciary—prove the rule: all other social institutions must be private to work best. Markets, like enterprises, should be "free," i.e., not subject to government.

Neoliberal politicians decline to organize, endorse, or support governmental production, import, storage, securing, or stockpiling of virtually anything that private capitalists are or could be doing instead. Private profit, not bureaucratic fiat, should be the guiding goal of the production and distribution of all goods and services (more or less excepting military, police, and judiciary). Libertarianism is a more extreme version of neoliberalism.

Where neoliberalism is strong, governmental preparations for and copings with coronavirus were weak, too late, and too little: as in the U.S., the UK, and Italy, among others. In societies where neoliberalism is relatively weak, government is accorded considerable respect and deference. Its anti-viral initiales and policies including economic interventions were welcomed or at least expected to play positive roles. Examples include China, South Korea, and New Zealand, among others. Where neoliberalism is weak, government economic interventions can receive ad hoc criticisms and oppositions, but they are not opposed in principle. Where neoliberalism is strong, opponents define government as always and necessarily an inefficient intruder into what private enterprise, if left alone, would do better.

Neoliberalism is a preferred ideology of private capitalist employers. This "special interest"—a very small social minority—embraces neoliberalism in self-interest. Its neoliberalism proclaims private capitalists' utter superiority to any other social group that threatens or might threaten its economic dominance. It thus excoriates labor unions and government bureaucracies and, sometimes, the monopolization of big businesses for interfering in and distorting free markets.

Neoliberalism views some government economic interventions as distorting intrusions into private capitalism; it views others as comprising an evil alternative to private capitalism. The label "socialism" serves neoliberals nicely to capture both horrors. On the one hand, it designates government meddling in free-market capitalism. On the other, it signifies government-owned and operated enterprises and government-planned distribution of resources and products. As private capitalism's chief theoretical champion, neoliberalism seeks to vanquish the enemy theories of Marx and Keynes.

Whatever we think of the theoretical jousting, coronavirus has sharply clarified neoliberalism's profound social costs. Millions are sick and many thousand dead because of governments' delayed and inadequate compensations for private capitalism's failures to prepare for or cope with the virus. Dangerous viruses have attacked human society many times throughout history. Preparing for the next attack—thereby securing public health—has long been a basic duty of all social systems. Feudalism failed in that duty when many millions of Europeans succumbed to the Black Death in the 14th century. That failure weakened European feudalism. Capitalism is failing in that duty now with coronavirus, in part because of neoliberalism.

As that lesson sinks in to contemporary consciousness, major challenges confront and will likely also weaken both neoliberalism and capitalism.

This article was published and syndicated by the Independent Media Institute's Economy for All project on May 29, 2020.

US Prepares for War, Not for COVID-19

July 5, 2020
Wolff Responds

I would like to compare how the United States handled the COVID-19 pandemic and how the United States handles military preparedness and military activity. There's more to be learned from this comparison than you might imagine.

Here's the problem, very simply. Viruses are an old, well understood problem. They have attacked human beings for as long as there has been a species called human beings. What you need to handle them is testing to see who's got it and who doesn't; and you need the equipment and the arrangements to prevent people from infecting one another. So, in order to have the public health protected, you need to have a proper stock of tests, masks, gloves, ventilators, hospital beds, the whole business of managing a virus when it attacks. Private companies cannot afford to produce huge quantities of these, to stockpile them around the country so they will be available to serve the populations that will need them. There is too much risk and too little profit in holding medical supplies in warehouses for months, or years, until they are purchased to deal with a virus. So private capitalist companies don't do it.

Now here is the parallel with defense spending. The same thing applies to guns, bullets, missiles, tanks, aircraft, and all the rest of military equipment. It doesn't pay for a company to produce jet fighters, for example, stockpile them in hangers around the United States, and wait for the next foreign crisis when the military comes to buy such equipment. That's too risky. Private capitalists may have to wait a long time, so they find less risky and more profitable opportunities.

If you leave capitalism to itself (to its private enterprises driven by profit), you will not get the production and stockpiling of the needed equipment to combat a virus and you will not get the production and stockpiling of the military equipment to fight wars.

Now let's see how these two problems have been resolved, or not, in the United States. Let's start with defense. The government doesn't say so, but here's what's going on: the government came in and solved the problem. It isn't profitable for private firms to produce guns, missiles, and tanks, so the government comes in and makes it profitable for them. The government agrees to purchase the goods as fast as they are produced, to take the risk onto itself. The government stockpiles these weapons around the country, indeed around the world, and maintains them at its own expense. If they go out of date because new weapons are developed, the government scraps the old and buys the new. The government promises private enterprises that they will make a lot of money because they will pay well for this military equipment. And so, we have guns, planes, missiles and tanks stockpiled all over the place.

Now, compare this to our medical preparation. Nothing. The government didn't do it. The government didn't do in the medical field what it did in the military field. It didn't buy and stockpile testing equipment, or the components of tests. It didn't stockpile and buy masks, ventilators, hospital beds, ICU's and all the rest of what we need. So, there wasn't any. The government didn't come in and admit that private capitalism can't and won't do it, and take the responsibility.

So the question becomes, what happened here? Don't we need to be protected from a virus at least as much as we need to be protected from some military activity directed against the United States? Of course we do. But the government didn't act, didn't do for the medical field what it does regularly for the defense field. And why not? And the answer is: the medical industries don't want it.

The medical industries can make more money doing other things. More importantly, they don't like the image of the government making up for the failure of private capitalist enterprises to do what public health demands. The very image that we need the government to secure public health because private enterprise in capitalism can't or won't do it is a problem they don't want to see underscored in our society at all.

The government didn't act in the medical area the way it does in the military to serve the private medical establishment: the doctors, the hospitals, the drug and device makers, and the medical insurance companies. Those four industries acting together made sure, as they always have, that the government is kept out of medicine. They always denounce government intervention in medical care as "socialism." Lots of their money has been spent buying lots of politicians, so the United States doesn't get the kind of medical system that every other advanced, industrial country has, despite the fact that we, in America, end up paying more for medical care than anyone else in the world.

We have a medical system limited and constrained by a private capitalist system that dominates and does not permit the government to do for medical preparedness what it does for military preparedness. Is it crazy to have a system like this? You bet. And the conclusions to be drawn from this, I will leave to you.

This essay has been adapted from "Wolff Responds: US Prepares for War, Not for COVID-19" posted on Professor Wolff's YouTube channel on July 5, 2020.

Why Government Mostly Helps People Who Need It the Least—Even During a Crisis

July 17, 2020
Independent Media Institute

In January 2020, the NASDAQ stock market's index stood just under 10,000. In the March crash, it fell to 7,000. As of July 10, 2020, it hit 10,600. The U.S. government's economic policies produced a "recovery" for the rich who own the vast bulk of stocks. Their holdings are worth more now than before COVID-19 hit us. The other major benchmarks for securities, the Dow Jones Industrial Average and the Standard and Poor 500, show similarly dramatic, slightly smaller recoveries.

Massive government economic intervention—what most of its current beneficiaries have always denounced—subsidized those recoveries. The Federal Reserve pumped unprecedented amounts of new money into the U.S. economy after mid-March. That money poured into the stock market and fueled its rise. The U.S. Treasury provided unprecedented direct cash supports to much of corporate America.

Over the same time, government economic support for the working class was too little, too late, and totally inadequate to what could and should have been done. In their unequal impacts, government economic policies were cruel and unjust. In this, they resemble government public health policies. With under 5 percent of the world's population, the United States accounts for about 25 percent of COVID-19 cases and about 24 percent of COVID-19 deaths globally. All but the most ideologically blinded (and government supporters) know what such a statistic means.

I focus here on how the government's economic policies affected corporations versus employees, the rich versus the middle class and the poor. Direct government support sustained most corporations. Bigger and richer corporations hire more and better lobbyists, make larger actual or potential donations to politicians and parties, and so on. They thus got big portions of government help. In general, the pandemic and crash hurt medium and small businesses more than big ones, while the latter got disproportionate government help. Government policies likely worsened the relative decline of small and medium businesses. Concentration and monopolization tendencies within U.S. capitalism strengthened.

The U.S. government's monetary policies (executed by the Federal Reserve) undertook to rescue the stock market as priority number 1. The Fed pumped in massive amounts of new money via very low-interest loans to banks and by directly buying corporate debt and U.S. government debt. In a collapsed economy with tens of millions of unemployed, little of that new money flowed into productive investments, rehiring workers, or enterprise expansions. Those did not offer attractive profits. Instead, the new money went where profits could still be made: the stock markets. Hence, they recovered.

Banks, corporations, and the rich used most of the new money to buy stocks from one another. That drove up stock prices. Each purchase by one Fed beneficiary was later sold to another Fed beneficiary at a higher price. Such capital gains encouraged repetitions or "stock flipping" (rather like real-estate hustlers' "house flipping" before the 2008 mortgage collapse crisis). As this stock market bubble continues to build, anxiety about eventual bursting rises.

Recoveries for corporations and the rich were not matched by what government policies achieved for most employees. The differences were stark. Employers fired more than 40 million employees who were thus forced to file for unemployment benefits. The government did not rehire those millions (to undertake COVID-19 testing of the U.S. population, a Green New Deal for infrastructure, etc.). The unemployed faced mounting difficulties in meeting their financial obligations.

Neither GOP nor Democratic leaders generated anything like the set of government programs that saved the working class from greater catastrophe during the 1930s Great Depression. Then, FDR's New Deal included establishing Social Security to provide monthly checks for all over 65, federal unemployment insurance, a minimum wage, and a federal jobs program that employed many millions of those fired by private employers.

It wasn't just incomes that were lost by the millions who have been unemployed since March (losses usually far above the $1,200 check given many and the extra $600 per week for the insured unemployed). No guarantee was provided that their old jobs would be available to them again or that their eventual wages and benefits would be what they were before COVID-19. When would their unemployment insurance fall or end? If they refused to return to unsafe workplaces (given that most Americans have still not been tested for COVID-19), would they lose jobs and eligibility for unemployment insurance? Excruciating anxiety added to the other sufferings of being unemployed in pandemic America. Many millions of unemployed now face near certainty that their former jobs are forever gone. They have thus lost the seniority, work relationships, connections, skills, and links to home, community, children's' schools, etc., that those jobs entailed.

Those who kept their jobs so far are nevertheless also threatened by today's mass unemployment. Employers can now confront their employees with wage and/or benefit reductions and other deteriorations of working conditions. If employees refuse, they risk getting fired and replaced by the increasingly desperate unemployed. Since employees know that, most knuckle under. Recent U.S. Bureau of Labor Statistics reports confirm that wages are declining with further declines widely predicted. Others who kept jobs and incomes but performed them from home encountered all sorts of new difficulties and expenses. For example, full-time air conditioning for stay-at-home workers and/or their children added hundreds of dollars to millions of affected workers' monthly utility bills.

Social movements across the country—Black Lives Matter, activism against eviction and for rent moratoria, strikes and job actions for COVID-19-safe working conditions, calls for debt relief, etc.—all attest to serious suffering and growing pushback. Those movements represent the other side of the recovery celebrations among corporations and the rich and the politicians and media they own. Rising stock markets and corporate bailouts—their recoveries—enabled the already richest to become richer still. Jeff Bezos, the CEO of Amazon, added $24 billion to his already more than $100 billion personal wealth. Meanwhile, the U.S. working class remains far, far from any comparable "recovery." Inequality in the United States deepens yet again.

Lest I be misunderstood or confused with libertarians, I do not attach responsibility for government policies primarily to politicians and bureaucrats. The government mostly does what its constituents with money and power make it do. In U.S. capitalism, most of the money and power are concentrated in a small minority: the corporate rich and their closest subordinates and allies. Occupy Wall Street referred to them as the 1 percent. Their interests prevail in government policies unless and until a genuinely countervailing power emerges from an organized mass of employees. Our big problem is not the government but the concentrated wealth and power that drive and control it.

Above all, it is the economic system—the division in production, inside almost all enterprises, between a minority of employers profiting from a majority of employees—that concentrates wealth and power. The needs and demands of that concentrated wealth and power dominate what "our" governments do and do not do. The system is the problem.

This article was published and syndicated by the Independent Media Institute's Economy for All project on July 17, 2020.

How the Fed Serves Capitalism

July 4, 2020
Ask Prof Wolff

The Federal Reserve ("The Fed") is the Central Bank of the United States and was created in 1913. It is their job, roughly, to keep price stability so we don't have inflation on the one hand, and deflation on the other. They also manipulate the American money supply so there's enough money to keep the economy going in a reasonable way, but not too much so that inflation happens. Finally, we've wanted the Federal Reserve to help moderate the business cycles, i.e., these terrible downturns, recessions, depressions, crashes, and busts, that occur every four to seven years and are so personally difficult, painful, costly, and disruptive.

The Federal Reserve is a creature of capitalism. It had to be established by the Congress and signed into law by the President. The corporate sector of our economy, always the dominant influence, was behind it. It was created to serve the reproduction of capitalism, and that is what it does to this day.

What is the Fed's record? It has kept prices, often, from going off the rails. We'll never know if the prices would've gone crazy if it hadn't been for the Federal Reserve. That might have happened, and there certainly were times when the Federal Reserve tried to stop it, and it didn't work. The record of the Federal Reserve on price stability is mixed. But it looks as though it helped some, and so there's no reason not to continue to have it monitor prices and try to intervene by adding or subtracting from the money supply to keep the prices from sharp inflations or deflations.

When it comes to their ability to interfere in business cycles and moderate them, the Fed's record is spottier. If anyone imagined that the Federal Reserve would eliminate business cycles, then you're looking at a total failure, as they haven't been able to do that. We're in a terrible one now, and it's the third one of this new century. Clearly, the Federal Reserve can't prevent, and doesn't look like it's really good at moderating, our business cycles. The one in 2008 and the one now, are among the worst five in the endless cycles that have characterized capitalism for over three centuries.

Well then, what can we say about the Federal Reserve? Firstly, it doesn't make much sense to focus your anger, upset or opposition on that part of the system. It was created by the capitalist system, its problems are those of the capitalist system, and it has had a mixed record of doing what it was designed to do, i.e., manage those problems or at least keep them from destroying the system. Nothing was ever expected or given to the Federal Reserve to control or shape what's going on.

Some of you will say, isn't it having a big influence now? The answer is yes, it is. That's partly why you're asking the question, and partly why it's getting so much attention. But that's not chiefly because the Federal Reserve is doing new and different things. It's more because the capitalist system is facing new, different, and much deeper problems.

We've had cycles every four to seven years, but the last two, the one in 2008 and the one now, are among the worst in our history. The Federal Reserve has a big role to play, because the problems it is supposed to solve are bigger than they ever have been. One of the major responses of the Federal Reserve to the crash in 2008 and now the crash in 2020 has been to do what they have always done, dropping interest rates. The interest rates have been dropped to help the economy by making it cheaper for corporations to borrow to invest, for individuals to borrow to buy a car or home, etc. We've dropped them not just a little, but virtually to zero. We have even flirted with negative interest rates. It's an extreme action, but it's in response to an extreme problem.

The Federal Reserve also has the power to create money, be it to print the bills we carry in our wallet or create financial accounts at banks out of nothing, which they have the right to do. These activities, leading to an increase in the money supply, have been extraordinary, going into the trillions of dollars. We've never done that before, but that's because US capitalism's problems are worse than they have been. The Federal Reserve pumped in wild amounts of money back in 2008, and even wilder amounts today.

Let's follow the money. The money goes into the hands of bankers and large corporations, and is then supposed to trickle down to the rest of us. That's long been the theory. The trickle down will help the economy get through whatever difficulty it faces.

What are corporations and banks doing? Is trickle down working? Let's start by making clear what they're not doing. They're not hiring large numbers of people. Why? Because they can't sell what they've already produced. They know that when we have over 40 million unemployed, people can and will buy less. Then too, real wages in the US have been stagnant for 40 years. The only reason we've been able to buy more is because of the debt the mass of Americans were willing to take on. But they can't take on much more debt, they're massively unemployed, and wages continue to go nowhere. So, there's no point in corporations, whose goal is to make profit, to take the free money they're getting from the Federal Reserve and invest it by hiring people to produce more. They have no interest in doing that, and as long as we allow their profit-based decisions to govern what happens, that's the outcome we will have.

So, the corporations are not going to invest in hiring people, and they're not going to invest in buying new machinery, or any of the other things that have to do with production—with the real-life economy of all of us who go to work, want to earn money, want to buy things, etc. They're not in the business of making the economy work well. They are in the business of making a profit for their corporation.

Then where does all the money go? It goes into the one place where corporations and banks can still profit these days—the stock market, where you can buy a share of stock, hold it for a few weeks or months, and then sell it to someone else (hopefully at a higher price) who's doing the same thing you did. The difference between what you paid for a share and what you get when you sell it (called a capital gain) is your profit.

All that extra money has, in fact, produced inflation, which is what the Federal Reserve always worries about. However, it's not an inflation in terms of our wages, and not an inflation in terms of goods and services we buy. A big inflation has happened in the stock market, and for the 10% of the people who own 85% of the shares, this is good news until the stock market's inflationary bubble bursts again. For the vast majority of Americans who own nothing or next to nothing in terms of shares, for whom today's economy is a source of fear, loss, and anxiety, Fed policy provides little help.

But the Federal Reserve doesn't care. It never did. Its job is not to help the mass of people. Its job is to keep the capitalist system going. That's a system that has produced inequality and instability, long before there was a Federal Reserve. The Federal Reserve isn't going to stop that process. That's not what it was established to do.

My conclusion: Don't waste your energy, your intellect, and your activism on the Federal Reserve. It doesn't deserve it. It is a creature and a servant of the capitalist system. That's our problem. It's a system in which a tiny group of people sit at the top of every business (e.g., the owner, the board of directors, etc.) and makes all the decisions—whether you have a job or not, what the company produces, how it produces, where it produces, and what is done with the profits you all helped to produce. That's the problem, and "our" government serves that system.

Capitalism, the system, is the problem. The Federal Reserve is not. It's a mere institution within, and serving that system, which is the problem.

This essay has been adapted from "Ask Prof Wolff: How the Fed serves Capitalism" posted on Democracy at Work's YouTube channel on July 4, 2020.

Capitalist Reality vs Conservative Ideology

July 11, 2020
Wolff Responds

Recent news reports have exposed a certain scandal surrounding the government's Payroll Protection Program (PPP), a government stimulus effort to help small businesses now that capitalism has crashed here in the United States. The scandal concerns the fact that the very people who've been specializing over the last 30 years (if not much longer) in attacking the government as an economic burden, unnecessary, inadequate, inappropriate, etc., have now been exposed for rushing to this payroll protection program for free money. Those taking government handouts now include the press secretary of president Trump as well as his close family members and his political cronies.

I liked most the application by the Ayn Rand Institute, an institute developed around the personality and work of one of the loudest conservative writers ever to have set foot here in the United States. The libertarian, anti-government Ayn Rand Institute got somewhere between $1-2 million out of this governmental program.

The president's press secretary, Kayleigh McEnany, was quoted as having celebrated removing welfare recipients from getting government money on the grounds that it is important to wean them away from governmental dependence. For her, the way you wean them away is to deny them a job, decent salary, and appropriate housing. For her, the best way to help someone in need is to take away their benefits. This same press secretary is one of many conservatives who advocate against the government and then fall all over themselves to get the government's money. McEnany's parents received $1-$2 million in PPP loans for their company, despite having more than 100 employees, and thus not qualifying for a "small business" loan.

There is a certain humor attached to their being exposed this way. It's sort of like capitalism refuting the conservatives who are trying so desperately to support it. They have gone so over the top that the system itself smacks them in the face as if to say "Hey, take it easy."

But that's not the part of the scandal that concerns me. The conservative community lives in a world other than the one that real capitalism lives in. The conservative community believes in a kind of capitalism that exists mostly in the textbooks of college economics courses, and in the minds and fantasies of conservatives. This kind of capitalism doesn't need the government, doesn't want the government, and thinks the government should be minimal if not totally eliminated from society.

But the reality is that the government has been a central support for capitalism throughout its history, and I want to go through a few of the ways in which the government has always been crucial to supporting capitalism.

Money makes the world go around more in capitalism than in any other system. A few centuries ago, early capitalists tried to let the money supply be controlled and run as a private enterprise. That didn't work out so well. Why? Because the people who got their hands on the control of money, mostly bankers, abused their control so badly that in the end the society and even the bankers understood you couldn't leave it in private hands.

And do you know who got the job of controlling the money supply? The government. In capitalist nations, central banks operated by the government control the nation's money supply.

In the US, we have the Federal Reserve, a partnership of government and banks. The Fed controls the money supply and has a big influence on shaping interest rates. We live in a society where the government has a major influence on the money supply and on interest rates, and thereby exerts a major influence on how the capitalist system works.

Banks were not the only ones who abused their private capitalist positions to make money at everybody else's expense. Three industries did it so badly that the government took control of them decades ago: banks, insurance, and utilities (electricity, gas, water, etc.).

The government tells these industries how much they can charge which limits their profits. Every one of the 50 states have a utilities commission to control that industry. It's the same with insurance. The government controls all of that to a limited extent because private capitalism can't be trusted. The system produces such contradictions, anger, bitterness and struggle that the government has to be brought in because the system left to itself would explode.

But there are other ways that the government supports capitalism. The federal government in this country purchases $750 billion worth of military equipment. It gives military producers huge contracts, virtually guaranteeing their profitability. What a wonderful thing for them. They have one customer and that customer takes good care of them. By this standard alone the government is crucial to an economy if it spends $750 billion just on the military. To not look at the role of the government in supporting countless industries and countless communities with its purchases is naive.

Here's another example. When people can't get work (we have millions of those) the government intervenes and gives them various kinds of support. If you didn't do that those people would become desperate. The government does not hire them because that would be competitive with the private sector, which opposes it. The government simply gives them an unemployment check. This is wise because if these people have nothing to lose, then who knows what might happen.

For another example, take public education. The government educates the vast majority of people. Not just K-12, but the roughly 75% of college students are educated in public colleges and universities. The government pays a big portion of the bills necessary for those institutions to work. This education means that the workers are much more productive employees of private capitalists than they would be otherwise. This saves the private capitalist employer the cost of educating and training much of the labor force they employ. It's a direct subsidy to capitalist employers, isn't it?

Sure, private enterprises can pick at the edges. Charter schools can offer to run their own operations, but what they really want is the government to pay for it. That's what the charter school movement among religious fundamentalists is all about. They want the government to pay, but they want to teach their particular religion to their particular audiences. It's not a general argument about what the state does or doesn't do because when they set up their little private schools, they look for and demand and fight all the way to the Supreme Court to get the government to pay for them.

The notion of capitalism without government is a utopian fantasy. It never existed, it has no prospect of existing, and it is a peculiarly weird concept now that everybody, including the Ayn Rand Institute, has their hand out for the government to save them. The next time you hear someone spout conservative notions about the benefits of small or no government, recognize it for the smokescreen it is, a way to pretend that capitalists haven't always relied on government to serve them.

This essay has been adapted from a "Wolff Responds: Capitalist Reality vs Conservative Ideology" posted on Professor Wolff's YouTube channel July 11, 2020.

Part III

Capitalism and Pandemic:
Social Illnesses that Affect Us All

How Capitalism and Racism Support Each Other

April 27, 2016
Truthout

"Racism" is so often applied to US prison statistics and policing; to data on differences in employment, housing, wealth and income distributions, college enrollments, film awards, and so much more; and to hardening hostilities toward immigration. At the same time, racism is so often condemned — at least in mainstream media, dominant political circles and most intellectual and academic institutions. Racism's persistence where the capitalist economic system prevails raises the question of the connection between capitalism and racism.

Many societies are structured and operate to subordinate one or more portions of their population — politically, culturally, economically or in combinations of these ways — while privileging others. Among the successive generations born into societies with such subordinations, some will challenge and seek to change their condition. Force can try to maintain subordination, but it is costly, dangerous and often unsuccessful. The preferred method has rather been (a) to develop an idea that justifies the subordination and (b) to install that idea as deeply as possible into the thinking of both the subordinated and the privileged.

One such idea is "race," the notion that sets of inherent (often deemed "natural") qualities differentiate groups of people from one another in fundamental ways. This idea of race can then be used to explain the subordination of some and the privileges of others as effects of their racial differences. The concept of race thus accomplishes a reversal: Instead of being a produced idea, an ex-post justification of structures of social subordination, race morphs instead into some pre-existing "reality" that caused or enabled the subordination.

We know how and why racism worked often to support slavery around the world and especially in the early United States. Masters endorsed and promoted ideas that justified slaves as subordinated because they were an inferior race. Racist ideology also sometimes supported feudalism by dividing lords and serfs into different races. Indeed, some early capitalist systems likewise racially distinguished employers from employees.

However, capitalism presents a more complex case, because it often made "individual freedom" central to its supportive ideologies. Opponents of slavery could use that ideology to fight for slavery's abolition. Yet capitalism's history nonetheless keeps exhibiting both the idea of race and racism. And the evidence marshaled by, among others, Manning Marable in How Capitalism Underdeveloped Black America (1983) certainly documents capitalism's subordination of many African Americans. Do racism and capitalism then support one another as per Malcolm X's famous statement, "You can't have capitalism without racism"? Should we follow Adolph Reed Jr.'s perspective (in his 2013 New Labor Forum article "Marx, Race and Neoliberalism") that sees racism as a "historically specific ideology that emerged, took shape, and has evolved as a constituent element within" capitalism?

Answers to these questions emerge from patterns exhibited by capitalism's inequality and instability. Capitalists never could end their system's tendency to generate gross inequality (in wealth and income distributions) nor its instability (in cycles of depression and recession). Both those features of capitalism have contributed to ongoing social injustice and oppositional social movements. Had the heavy burdens of recurring business cycles (periodic unemployment and its multiple consequences) been distributed roughly equally or randomly across societies where capitalism prevailed — threatening and frightening everyone — those oppositional movements might well have gathered the broad support needed to consign capitalism to an early demise.

However, those burdens were never distributed equally or randomly. Some suffered them disproportionally and repeatedly, resulting in social subordination. Others were relatively privileged, exempted from those burdens partially or totally. Yet, in their struggles to displace slavery and feudalism as societies' prevalent pre-capitalist economic systems, supporters of capitalism had often promised that it would differ from those systems by guaranteeing everyone liberty, equality and brotherhood or solidarity. What capitalism achieved contradicted that promise.

The burdens of capitalism's instability fell much harder on employees than employers, and much harder upon some employees than others. Capitalism thus always faced a basic legitimation problem. How could it justify its unequal distributions of income, wealth and the burdens of its systemic instability among the people whose condition of being "free and equal" capitalism was supposed to guarantee?

One of the major means of managing this legitimation problem has been an ideology of race (alongside other ideologies centered around concepts such as "productivity" and "meritocracy"). Capitalism repurposed race and racism. By dividing human beings, conceptually and practically, into intrinsically different subgroups, capitalism's defenders could explain and justify why its economic benefits (e.g. the status of employer rather than employee) and burdens (unemployment, poverty etc.) were so unequally distributed (both within countries and globally). Employers, politicians, academics and journalists reinforced the notion that the cause, fault or blame for that unequal distribution lay with racially differentiated characteristics, not with the capitalist system.

Certain population groups — conceived as races — were deemed underdeveloped, incapable, irrational and/or psychologically disqualified in relation to capitalism's productive rigors. Such presumed inferiority was then offered as an explanation for why people of some races were rarely employers and, among employees, were those last hired and first fired, poorly paid, ghettoized etc.

Such races — often non-whites — were, in effect, assigned to play the role of shock absorbers in and for capitalist business cycles. They still are: A 2016 report from the University of Illinois, using the racialized differentiations, documents how young people of color in the United States continue to face significantly higher rates of unemployment and lower employment per population ratios than young white people do.

In the United States, most white employees have been spared constantly fearing and periodically suffering unemployment and its consequences. A minority of white employees shares the fate of a huge portion of the "shock absorber" races. That fate comprises job insecurity, recurring unemployment and its consequences: loss of skills, job connections and promotions; descent into hopelessness and desperation; turning toward illegal revenue-generating activities; policed into disproportionate incarceration; etc. By concentrating both poverty and the business cycle shock absorber role in certain subgroups of their populations and by using racism to explain that concentration, capitalist societies "manage" the risks attending their tendencies to gross inequality and instability.

Some conservatives and right-wingers further legitimate capitalism by reframing their racism. For them "the problem" is that capitalism has not been allowed to work its healing magic — market discipline — upon those inferior groups. Misguided social protections, minimum wages, safety nets, welfare etc. have kept them inside a "culture of poverty" defined as recurring unemployment, poverty, social isolation, family instability, incarceration etc. By correcting (i.e. removing) those misguided and counterproductive social protections, capitalism's disciplines would integrate them into prosperity and growth. That this has not happened for most subordinate groups is blamed on the depth of their racialized inferiority and/or the legacy of liberals' imposition of a culture of poverty.

In contrast, liberals and social democrats who accept the concept of race have mostly sought to ameliorate the sufferings of the unemployed and poor by policies such as education, welfare and training. Such policies likewise rarely succeeded either generally or enduringly. They could not overcome the system's reproduction of poverty and unemployment and the imposition of them disproportionally on the shock absorber "races." Both conservatives and liberals have enforced a shared denial of the mechanisms of mutual support between capitalism and racism.

Of course, capitalism is not the only cause or source of racism, but ignoring or minimizing its role only perpetuates racism. By designating some members of society to be shock absorbers of recurring business cycles, the capitalist system creates legacies of trauma and inequality that can accumulate into dysfunctional qualities for its victims. There is neither need nor warrant to take those qualities as givens, nor to transform them into racialized attributes. The solution is rather to treat those legacies as among the profoundly unacceptable consequences and costs of capitalism's profoundly divisive inequality and instability.

A capitalism that perpetuates itself via racism incurs huge self-protection costs: to police and imprison or to provide some safety nets for its shock absorber "races" or varying combinations of both. When capitalists shift some or all of those costs onto the tax obligations of workers, more social tensions emerge. Workers are then told their tax payments must compensate for the "deficiencies" attributed to the shock absorber "races" rather than to the structural irrationalities of capitalism. Racial conflicts then preclude or tear apart working-class political unity. Racism persists in no small part because its benefits to capitalism outweigh its costs, or at least those costs capitalists have to bear.

When capitalists and their ideological supporters disavow racism, they carefully ignore capitalism as a key part of the problem. They point instead to the intolerance of "some people who lack compassion for the less fortunate." Thereby they further divide the working class, in effect, into one race that cannot or will not work hard (and is therefore unemployed and poor) and another race that lacks compassion. In comparison, capitalists and their supporters congratulate themselves for their superior morality.

Capitalism thus comes full circle. Its supporters use and benefit from a racism whose practice and consequences they blame exclusively on others but never on capitalism itself.

This article was published in Truthout on April 27, 2016.

The Capitalism/Racism Partnership

July 18, 2018
Common Dreams

In the wake of W.E.B. DuBois 's 150th birthday, his works offer a lens through which to assess US capitalism's relationship to racism today. He famously wrote: "Capitalism cannot reform itself; it is doomed to self-destruction," while adding that in the US, race would be a key issue in that process. Thus, he would have had much to say when, around last Memorial Day, Trump suggested that NFL players peacefully protesting police killings of black people did not belong "in the country."

An extreme right-wing capitalist agenda prevails. It pushes private capitalists' goals—privatization and deregulation; tax cuts for corporations and the rich; and subsidies for them—to lengths not seen before. A kind of unhinged capitalist euphoria makes a virtue of learning nothing about restraint from the catastrophic booms and busts associated with 1929 and 2008.

Capitalism's headlong rush is quite logically symbolized and figureheaded by Trump. Yet what makes it possible is above all the absence of any serious, organized opposition such as that successfully mounted during the Great Depression by the New Deal coalition of industrial unions, two socialist parties, and one communist party. After 1945, Republicans attacked and Democrats abetted the demise of the New Deal Coalition and subsequent efforts to rebuild it. That allowed a capitalist resurgence and thereby the resumption yet again of another drive to crisis. When that happened in 2008-2009, the absence of a serious left opposition precluded anything like another New Deal. After 2008 we had only bailouts (much bigger than FDR's in the 1930s). Oblivious to capitalism's history, today's centrist Democratic Party leadership waits for Trump's demise so it can resume the Clintons' legacy: another drive to crisis.

While no broad-based national opposition yet exists in the US, there are signs of it struggling to be born. Public school teachers—some with and some without union supports—became active finally against years of public school funding cutbacks accelerated under the grotesque DeVos administration. The striking teachers' success in West Virginia showed what serious, organized opposition can do. Likewise, the high-schoolers from Parkland, Florida, organized opposition to the gun lobby, mocking the fakeries and lip-service of so many others. Consider too the proliferating organizations of and for worker coops as a democratic alternative to undemocratically organized capitalist enterprises.

There are more examples, but what matters basically is this: social change requires serious, organized opposition to the status quo. The further the social change seeks to go, the better organized its proponents within that serious opposition need to be. Defeating a particular politician takes less organizing than defeating a political party and that, in turn, takes less than making a transition to a better, different economy.

DuBois understood that capitalism's drive to self-destruction would eventually prompt last-ditch efforts to save the system. We see these now in the sorts of extreme deregulation, tax cuts for business and the rich, etc. undertaken by the Trump regime. The bubble and subsequent recession to which they are building plus the extreme income and wealth inequalities that they worsen are signals of impending serious opposition. So too are the efforts to distract attention from system-critique and toward selected scapegoats, non-white immigrants especially. Revulsion is building towards the smokescreens of hypocrisy, racism, and nationalism barely masking capitalism's ongoing failure to provide the jobs and incomes people need.

DuBois split his political efforts between appealing to African-Americans to embrace anti-capitalism and to socialists to embrace anti-racism. In his view, no program to establish socialism in the US could succeed or survive so long as African-Americans were kept as employees or unemployed. Likewise, no program to abolish racism was possible within the US capitalist system.

Racism in the US had settled deeply into the economics, politics and culture of the US since its inception. It had adjusted itself to capitalism and vice-versa. Their interdependence or partnership was deeply structured. Thus, for example, US capitalism could use racism to solve the problems of two of its worst features: instability and inequality. The business cycles ever besetting capitalism threatened the entire working class with periodic unemployment, poverty, etc. That constant threat—as well as the recurring downturns themselves—risked provoking working class opposition to capitalism as a system. Racism facilitated offloading instability's risks and costs onto the African-American community that was last hired, first fired. A large part of the white population could thus escape capitalism's instability or suffer less from it. Racist arguments then blamed African-Americans for their unemployment and poverty by contrasting it with that of most whites. Racism and capitalism reinforced one another in this way.

In parallel fashion, capitalism's incessantly rising inequality threatens the entire working class with relative and often also absolute poverty. Racism assigns African-Americans to the bottom of the income and wealth distributions (via racist hiring, housing, schooling, public policies, and attitudes). Many whites feel less threatened by capitalism's drive to ever greater inequality because a disproportionate share of that inequality is dumped onto the African-American community. Whites have a constant exhibit of "it could be worse" flowing from that community's living conditions.

A partnership between anti-capitalism and anti-racism within social movements and in public discourse could dissolve the mutual reinforcement between racism and capitalism and thereby advance progressive social change. Today's capitalism includes contradictions pushing toward that dissolution. Long-term wage stagnation and profit-driven technical changes are subjecting more and more whites to conditions previously limited largely to African-Americans. Hence the household disintegrations, drug dependencies, etc. long afflicting African-Americans are increasingly suffered among whites as well.

The resurgence of white-supremacy represents anxiety about descent into conditions that capitalism and racism had earlier let most whites escape. It is the other side of whites' recognizing their basic employee position within capitalism as shared with African-Americans. Capitalism's current development (the rush to privatize, cut taxes, export jobs, automate, etc.) drives conservatives (not just Trump) to cultivate white-supremacy against the growing working class solidarity the system itself generates. In the light of DuBois's concept of capitalism's "self-destruction," might today's polarizing politics (Trump), ideologies, culture and economy be its multiple signs?

This article was published in Common Dreams on July 18, 2018.

How Capitalism Has Screwed Women Over

October 31, 2018
Huffington Post

It's been one year since the explosion of the Me Too movement that followed allegations against Harvey Weinstein. Since then, the #metoo hashtag has been used around 19 million times to expose and discuss workplace sexual harassment.

Women are raising their voices. The struggle is multifaceted, but at its heart, women want economic and political equality with men. They also are increasingly questioning capitalism, the system that has allowed and maintained their subordination.

To understand how women have been systematically denied so much of what capitalism has provided to their male peers, we need to go back to a pre-capitalist age.

Before capitalism, there was feudalism — a social structure in which most people (serfs) worked for and answered to lords, who in return granted them land and protection. There was often little or no use of money. Lords did not hire workers. Instead, the subordination was personal and church-sanctioned. People were tied to the land on which they were born, and there wasn't the separation we take for granted today between work and home.

When the transition from feudalism to capitalism began, starting in 17th-century England before spreading globally, enthusiastic supporters promised the new economic system would bring the individual freedom, equality, social solidarity and democracy people longed for. The slogan of the French Revolution that overthrew feudalism was "liberty, equality, fraternity." To this, the American Revolution added "democracy."

For men, capitalism meant escape — from belonging to a lord, being tied to the land, and from rigid hierarchies. Now, they were free to sell their labor to whomever they wanted, without any moral or religious obligation. They relished their escape from feudalism, even as they found themselves trapped within capitalism's employer-employee relationship.

But most women were excluded from even the limited benefits that men enjoyed. Capitalism didn't provide decently paid employment for both men and women. The solution was to insist that women stay at home. A man's wage plus a woman's work in the home meant no mass of paid jobs needed to be available for women. Capitalists also managed to avoid paying for the child care that produced their future employees.

At home, women cooked meals; cleaned rooms, clothes, and dishes; repaired furniture; provided health care and child care. They worked like feudal serfs. Men's lives navigated daily between household feudalism and workplace capitalism. Exploited by capitalists at work, men could, in turn, exploit their wives at home. It's women's subordination inside households that has produced many of the inequalities, discriminations, and abuses women are protesting to this day.

Over the last century, huge numbers of women started to work outside the home, led by poorer women. World War II saw large numbers of women entering the workforce. Then, in the 1970s, automation and globalization ended the long tradition of rising real wages in the U.S. So, women entered the workplace to bring more money into the family. And, in doing so, they often shouldered the burdensome double shift of home and work. Women also tended to be funneled into "pink collar" jobs, such as retail, nursing or teaching, which were paid less.

All the while, across workplaces, women had to deal with men's competitive anxieties. This often manifested itself in men's attempts to extend household inequality to the workplace. As the Me Too movement makes clear, they still do, and the costs are heavy. But as women fight for equality with men, many have realized that the ultimate problem is not the men. Rather it is the system that has positioned men and women in an unequal economic relationship with employers that infects all the other aspects of their relationships.

There is a movement of women who want more than just to work alongside men within a capitalism that continues to subordinate and exploit them both.

To do that requires that we reorganize how we run homes and businesses in ways neither capitalist nor feudal. Instead, workplaces can be organized as democratic communities. One person, one vote, decides all key workplace matters. The premise of such "worker coops" is that the democracy Americans endorse for politics belongs as well in economics. Such a change could free women and men from being trapped in the system that serves neither.

This article was published in the Huffington Post on October 31, 2018.

Government Debts as Class Swindles

January 31, 2020
Common Dreams

In modern capitalism, governments routinely borrow money. They do this to finance budget deficits that occur when governments raise less in taxes than they spend. Governments also borrow to invest in long-term projects of economic development. The swindling occurs when the lenders and borrowers—usually private financiers and career politicians—negotiate loans that serve their own particular interests at the expense of the taxpayers who eventually cover the costs of repaying the government's loans plus interest on them.

If governments raised enough taxes to cover their desired levels of spending, they would not need to borrow. Taxes imposed on the wealthiest corporations and individuals would be the most equitable strategy. The corporate wealthy protest, of course, threatening that if taxed, they might reduce their contributions to the economy (investing less, etc.). Most government politicians sympathize with those protests. Many come from the ranks of the wealthiest corporations and individuals (or aspire to join them). They share similar ideologies and depend on campaign donations from them. Compliant politicians typically exaggerate the negative aspects of taxing corporations and the rich. They rarely compare them to the negative effects of the alternatives: taxing middle- and lower-income people more or cutting government spending.

Government borrowing to cover budget deficits has its own negative effects on the economy. Many variables influence the impacts of taxes and deficit borrowing. Because those variables' effects cannot be known or measured for years into the future, no one can know which is better or worse for the economy in the long run. When the corporate rich and their political allies stress the negative effects of taxes on the rich they usually carefully neglect the other side of the story as when advertisers mention only the positive side of whatever they are paid to promote. Their goals are simply more profits and less taxes.

The class swindle goes deeper than one-sided untruths about taxes. This becomes clear when we identify who lends to borrowing governments. Banks, big corporations, the 5% wealthiest individuals and other governments are the chief lenders. They are the same economic groups (excepting foreign governments) that press for and get tax cuts such as the Trump/GOP tax reduction of December 2017. That particular tax cut increased the federal budget deficit to over $1 trillion in 2019. The same politicians who facilitate tax reductions for banks, big corporations, and the wealthiest individuals likewise then facilitate government borrowing money from them.

The class swindle embedded in government borrowing is the none-too-subtle mechanism whereby the richest sectors of modern capitalism avoid or replace taxes levied on them with interest-bearing loans to the same government. What a deal for the rich who thus exchange taxes (assets lost) for loans (assets and income gained)! And what a deal for their political servants: leaders who can spend more to buy votes and secure donations without having to tax anybody because they can borrow instead. And by the time the mass of taxpayers watching all this grasps the swindle perpetrated on them, those leaders have moved up their political ladders. Their replacements will then respond to popular anger by ostentatiously raising taxes less or maybe even cutting them in favor of, yet again, borrowing. As this can gets kicked down the road, its explosive potential builds.

Deficit finance—the polite veneer for this swindle—deepens inequality in the United States and everywhere else it is practiced. It redistributes wealth from the mass of people (taxpayers) to the richest who "save" by means of lower taxes and then "invest" those "savings" in government loans. In transferring money from the many to a few, deficit finance operates like a lottery.

A different but parallel sort of swindle occurs when governments, especially in "emerging economies" (Asia, Africa, Latin America, and so on), borrow from banks and other lenders in the "advanced industrial economies." Here the perpetrators are, on the one side, bankers and other lenders eager to make profitable loans to foreign governments. On the other side are government politicians eager to borrow. The latters' eagerness flows from two sources. The first is the need to secure their political careers by funding economic development projects that could not otherwise occur because those politicians fear the electoral results of using taxes to pay for the projects. The second is their ability to divert, legally or otherwise, sizable portions of the loans they procure to finance themselves and their parties in addition to (or even instead of) their development projects.

These lenders and borrowers gather easily in expensive hotels to negotiate wondrous "development loans" nicely serving both their needs. The loans are backed, of course, by the borrowing country's ability to tax its citizens and/or sell its natural resources and/or sell its government operations to pay off the loans and the interest on them. Given such loans' high profitability, they can and often do run for years before outraged local citizens revolt and refuse to keep paying. Then the country declares bankruptcy amid threats and lamentations on all sides. Eventually, what remains of the loan is partly or wholly forgiven. No problem: the lenders' profits were already reaped, the career benefits achieved. Soon the whole process begins again.

The organization and manipulation of government debts (to finance budget deficits and development projects) have been core components of world capitalism's real history for centuries. The system fosters those swindles. The system also rejects or ignores the critics of those swindles including Modern Monetary Theorists, Marxists, and "populists" of varying persuasions. Change comes when finally, the swindle's critics and its victims merge to end it.

This article was published in Common Dreams on January 31, 2020.

The Rush to Get Americans Back to Unsafe Workplaces

April 24, and April 29, 2020
Wolff Responds

I want to talk to you about the accelerating rush to "put America back to work," or to "get the economy going again." Phrases like this are coming from the president and from leading CEOs, and I want to warn you about it. I want to make sure what's going here is understood.

We have a government and a private sector that failed catastrophically to prepare for this viral pandemic. The companies that make the masks, the ventilators, the tests, the gowns, the hospital beds, etc. didn't produce what we need, didn't import what we need, nor did they stockpile what we need around the country. They failed and so did the government that is supposed to compensate for the failures of private capitalism. Government failed because it so blindly supports private capitalism, believing that what is privately profitable is also socially efficient (and I'm talking about both the Republican and Democratic party establishments). So, we've had to lockdown because Americans are dying at a scale we've yet to see anywhere else.

And what is the response? Well, there are efforts to get the testing done. They're late, they're slow, and most of all, they're insufficient. The same is true of everything else: beds, ventilators, you name it. And in this situation, not only are there no abject apologies by the leaders of a system so spectacularly failing, but it's worse. There is now a rush for people to go back to work. That's what the reality is beneath the lofty phrases: "getting us back in gear" and "restarting the economy."

Capitalists have discovered an old economic lesson: you can have all the machines in the world, the latest technology, and the glitziest factories, but they're all worthless items unless human beings—workers—are in there using them, applying them, making things happen. So, capitalists need workers. The reverse, not so much. Everything those capitalists have, the machines, the buildings, the technology, you know who made them? Not those capitalists. Workers. That's right.

The capitalists realize they need workers, but the workers are all at home because they don't want to die from dangerous workplace conditions. They don't want to get the virus and infect their partners, children, elderly, neighbors, and friends. But the capitalists need profits and you can only get that if the workers are working. So now the rush is on: make the workers come back, plead with them, beg with them, tell them it's patriotic. Tell them it's their duty. Force them by telling them they won't get their unemployment check anymore, or their jobs back, and so on.

But don't be fooled. The failure of the capitalists isn't over. Most of them have done absolutely nothing in this moment to make their workplaces safer. Does the workplace have an ongoing testing department adequately equipped and staffed? Adequate testing doesn't just happen once. The testing has to go on over and over again at every workplace or else you are at risk. What about the masks? What about the ventilators? What about the beds? What about sick leave so that you can be taken care of if you do get sick? Has everything been reconfigured so you're at least six to nine feet away from the next person? In the bathrooms? At lunch? Where you change clothes? Have they done all that? Have they taken the steps? Who is going to monitor this?

And above all, because it's capitalism, have they paid for it? Most capitalists haven't done it. They don't want to do it, they don't want to pay for it. But they want you to come back anyway. How surprising.

It's unconscionable to pressure people to choose between going without a job on the one hand or risking their lives on the other. This choice exists because corporations don't want to spend money to do what has to be done, such as ongoing testing and tracing of people who test positive, constant disinfecting, and the reconfiguration of workplaces to accommodate social distancing.

None of that has been done adequately and until it has, you should not accept being forced to choose between a job or your life, especially not when the only thing holding us back from safe workplaces is corporate money.

There are movements all over the United States, groups of workers here and there, not willing to go back and risk their lives and that of their families. There is even talk of a general strike, which is when a whole working class says to the capitalists: "No, we will not work under the conditions you're trying to impose on us." It's happened before in history and it's something all of us should be thinking about now. If this rush to get us back to work continues, we are being asked to risk our lives to make profits for the capitalist class. Do you really want to be a part of that?

Whether or not a workplace opens has to be decided by all the people involved, not just by the corporate leadership at the top. They call all the shots and they make all the decisions because that's what the word "employer" means in capitalism. If ever you wanted a demonstration of how unacceptable and undemocratic capitalism is, we're in the middle of it now.

This ought to be a democratic decision. All workers are taking a chance if they go back to work, and all workers are taking a chance if they don't go back. Therefore, all workers should have an equal voice in deciding whether and when it's safe to go back. It's unacceptable to have some boss tell you, in effect, to risk your life because they were too cheap to make it safe.

This is not just a virus problem, and it's not just an economic crash. We are being brought face to face with the fact that capitalism is undemocratic; and capitalism is now threatening our lives. It's time to change the system.

This essay has been adapted from two "Wolff Responds" videos on Professor Wolff's YouTube channel: "Rush to get Americans Back to Work" posted on April 24, and "Return to Work Means a Return to Unsafe Workplaces" posted on April 29, 2020.

Mass Unemployment Is a Failure of Capitalism

May 8, 2020
Independent Media Institute

The difficulties caused to workers by record unemployment during the pandemic are a product of capitalism. Most of the time, employers decide to hire or fire workers depending on which choice maximizes employers' profits. Profit, not the full employment of workers nor of means of production, is "the bottom line" of capitalism and thus of capitalists. That is how the system works. Capitalists are rewarded when their profits are high and punished when they are not. It's nothing personal; it's just business.

Unemployment is a choice mostly made by employers. In many cases of unemployment, employers had the option not to fire employees. They could have kept all employed but reduced their hours or days or else rotated off-work times among employees. Employers can choose to retain idled employees on payrolls and suffer losses they hope will be temporary.

However, unemployment is received almost everywhere and by almost all as a negative, unwanted experience. Workers want jobs. Employers want employees producing profitable output. Governments want the tax revenues that flow from employees and employers actively collaborating.

So why has the capitalist system periodically produced economic downturns wherever it has settled across the last three centuries? They have happened, on average, every four to seven years. The United States has had three crashes so far this century: "dot-com" in 2000; "sub-prime mortgage" in 2008; and now "coronavirus" in 2020. Thus the United States conforms to capitalism's "norm." Capitalists do not want unemployment, but they regularly generate it. It is a basic contradiction of their system.

There are good reasons why capitalism produces and reproduces unemployment over time. It draws benefits (as well as suffers losses) from doing so. Reproducing a "reserve army of the unemployed" enables periodic upsurges in capital investment to draw more employees without driving up wages. Rising wages—and thus falling profits—would accompany investment surges if all workers were already fully employed before such surges. Unemployment also disciplines the working class. The unemployed, often desperate to get jobs, give employers the opportunity to replace existing employees with unemployed candidates willing to work for less.

Unemployment thus operates as a downward pressure on wages and salaries and thereby a boost for profits. In short, capitalism both wants and does not want unemployment; it expresses this tension by periodically adding to and drawing down a reserve army of the unemployed that it continually maintains.

That reserve army exposes a stark reality that no ideological gloss ever fully erases. While unemployment serves capitalism, it does not well serve society. That key difference is most glaringly in evidence when unemployment is very high, as it is today. Consider that today's many unemployed millions continue much of their consumption while ceasing much of their production. While they continue to take their means of consumption from socially produced wealth, they no longer produce nor thereby add to social wealth as they did when employed.

Unemployment thus entails wealth redistribution. Part of the wealth produced by those who are still employed must be redistributed away from them and to the unemployed. Taxes accomplish that redistribution publicly. Employees and employers, labor and capital struggle over whose taxes will fund the consumption of the unemployed. Such redistribution struggles can be and often are bitter and socially divisive. In the private sphere of households, portions of the incomes and wealth of the employed likewise get redistributed to enable consumption by the unemployed: spouses share, as do parents and children, relatives, friends, and neighbors. Working classes always redistribute their incomes and wealth to cope with the unemployment capitalism so regularly imposes on them. Such redistributions typically cause or aggravate many tensions and conflicts within the working class.

Many public and private redistribution struggles could be avoided if, for example, public re-employment replaced private unemployment. If the state became the employer of last resort, those fired by private employers could immediately be rehired by the state to do socially useful work. Governments would stop paying unemployment benefits and instead pay wages to the re-employed, obtain in return real goods and services, and distribute them to the public. The 1930s New Deal did exactly that for millions fired by private employers.

A similar alternative to private capitalist employment and unemployment (but not part of the New Deal) would be to organize the unemployed into worker co-op enterprises performing socially useful work on contract with the government.

This last alternative is the best because it could develop a new worker-co-op sector of the U.S. economy. That would provide the U.S. public with direct experience in comparing the capitalist with the worker-co-op sector in terms of working conditions, product quality and price, civic responsibility, etc. On that concrete, empirical basis, societies could offer people a real, democratic choice as to what mix of capitalist and worker-co-op sectors of the economy they prefer.

This article was published and syndicated by the Independent Media Institute's Economy for All project on May 8, 2020.

US Capitalism's Forced Labor

May 11, May 22, May 28, 2020
Wolff Responds

President Trump and his government have sent out a notice to all 50 state governments in the United States offering them "encouragement and guidance" – those are the words the notice used – to order "essential workers" back to work after lockdowns from COVID-19. But much more than that, the notice also basically said that if any employer asks (orders) his workers back to work and those workers refuse, not only would the employer be free to fire them, but the unemployment insurance that they were receiving, or might be eligible for, could be, and should be, withheld from them.

Now, you can dance up and down and left and right all you want, but you cannot dance around what this is. It has a name. It is called forced labor. It is forced labor to tell the American people that even though their employer may have done little or nothing to make the workplace safe, they must go to work if the employer chooses and that if they don't, they will be immediately reduced to poverty. They will lose their job, they will therefore lose their income, and they will be deprived of, or at least risk being deprived of, their unemployment insurance.

Notice the government and whose side it's on here. Orders have gone out now repeatedly from the highest authorities in the country ordering people back to work without any matching order for the employers to spend the money to make workplaces safe.

The Trump administration and the Republican Party have announced that they are going to demand a law to protect companies that are telling their workers they must come back to work. The law would limit companies' liability from any lawsuits that workers and customers might pursue against the companies for having unsafe workplaces. The companies can thus save money by not making their workplaces safe. This is extraordinary.

American working people are being forced to go back to work or there's going to be hell to pay. You can, of course, "choose" not to, and then you can suffer the job loss, the income loss, and possibly the lost unemployment insurance. What a "choice" for the capitalist system to give the majority of its people.

So, an already bad situation is even worse now. If you go back to work and you get the virus, bring it home and infect the family and possibly thereby kill another person, you will not be able to recover anything from the employer who put you in that position. Remember, when President Trump ordered the meatpackers back to work, he did not order their meatpacking employers to make their workplaces safe.

The Democrats haven't gone in that direction, which might make you a bit more sympathetic to them, but not necessarily. What the Democratic Party has been doing is pointing out that the 50 states are in terrible financial shape because unemployment means people don't pay taxes to the city or the state they live in. Cities and states need to do more for people when they're unemployed, but they get less revenue for it. It's the same kind of problem that, in effect, businesses have. But the Republican-dominated government, having bailed out businesses, is threatening not to bail out states and cities. Mitch McConnell, the Republican leader in the Senate, even went so far as to urge cities and states to go bankrupt, to not pay off their obligations, which include the tens of millions of public employees who have been paying into their pensions their entire lives.

So, here's what the Republicans have done. They've told the Democrats that they will not help cities and states unless the Democrats cave in and let them provide capitalist enterprises with limited liability protection in court against any suits from workers damaged by being forced to go back to work. All without the employer or the government having taken half of the steps that would be necessary to make the workplace safe.

Capitalism as a system has always ripped off the working class. Most workers know it. They know it if for no other reason than the bar they pass on the way home always invites them in for a "happy hour" because it knows that the hours at work weren't. But this takes it to a whole new level. You are going to be forced to go to work, you're going to have to bear the risk of illness and death, and you're going to have to accept that you can't go to court and recover for the horror that your employer has imposed on you. That is because the government has freed the employer from liability in court. If ever there was an economic system that no longer deserved the loyalty of the people living under it, we have now arrived at a capitalism that has brought us to just that point.

On May 5th, garbage collectors in New Orleans, Louisiana, went on strike, demanding an increase in their wages from $10.25 an hour to $15 an hour. Also, they wanted their trucks, used to collect garbage, fixed because they were dangerously broken. And they wanted protective equipment: masks, gloves, all of that. As one striker put it, "The garbage is full of items that carry the coronavirus. We are on the front lines of removing that from where it can infect other people, and we need to be protected ourselves."

98

What was the response of the officials in New Orleans, Louisiana, to this demand of frightened, underpaid, frontline, essential workers who were earning the poverty wage of $10.25 an hour for hard, dangerous work?

The city of New Orleans contracts with private services to take care of garbage collection. The private services in turn contract with temporary work agencies who provide the actual labor. The temporary agency in this case fired the striking workers. Did the garbage pile up with the workers fired? No, because the city of New Orleans, together with its contracting garbage collector, together with the temp agency that provided these workers, had a better plan. They brought over inmates from a prison in neighboring Livingston Parish, who were required to do this work. And they were paid, according to the state rules in Louisiana, the going rate for prison inmates, which is not $10.25 an hour. It is $1.33 per hour.

A wonderful saving for the temp agency, for the contracting garbage collector, and for New Orleans. These three employers – two private, one state – got together to replace workers for whom they did not want to spend the money to keep them whole and to keep them safe. Instead, they got prisoners for whom they had to make no such expenditure.

Are you horrified? I hope so. But this isn't more than the next step in the logic that drove President Trump to order the meatpackers back to work in the Midwest, even though they were showing up with an enormous percentage of workers carrying the coronavirus. Forced labor.

It is often said that capitalism, the system of employers and employees, depends on "voluntary agreements and contracts between employers and employees." Nothing is voluntary when you are forced by government order, or by order of the prison warden.

And let's not forget: Here in the United States, we put more people into prison per capita than any other country. Capitalism with forced labor. That's what's growing in the United States. And it's a sure sign that the levels of tension, conflict, anger, bitterness, and division are deepening. The days, the weeks, and the months of a capitalism that works this way are numbered.

We know that employers must literally be forced to protect their workers, because that is the history of capitalism. That's how and why we have the Occupational Safety and Health Administration here in the United States. That's why we struggled for and passed the Food and Drug Administration's legislation and dozens of other laws governing the control of meat and bread making, and every other aspect of our society's food chain, as well as many other parts of the economy.

We have forced labor now in the United States. Capitalism has become so desperate that it throws aside the polite veneer, revealing underneath what Jack London called the "iron fist of capitalism." There is no more enticing you to work with a good wage or good working conditions. No, no, no. We now have capitalist employers telling you, you either come to work here if we offer you a job or we're going to reduce you to nothing, economically – no job, no income, no unemployment insurance – forcing people to work. And suppose the employer cuts the wage, or suppose the employer changes the work pace. No, there's no rule that governs any of this. It's the same naked iron fist. You work or you suffer, right away and seriously.

There was a time not that long ago when Americans looked at other countries where they found forced or slave labor and were highly critical. Maybe Americans will continue to do that, but now they risk a response: Who are you calling names? Look to your own practices.

Making workers risk life-threatening infections they could take home to their families because employers have not chosen to spend the money to make workplaces safe, and have not been forced to by the government, is a reduction of the last little bits of freedom workers had. It's a sign of a capitalism that is not only in deep trouble but is becoming increasingly desperate, because the workers in the United States are beginning to understand what is happening also, and there will be repercussions.

This essay has been adapted from three "Wolff Responds" videos on Professor Wolff's YouTube channel: "Employer's Limited Liability" posted on May 11, "Trump's Executive Orders" posted on May 22, and "Forced Labor" posted on May 28, 2020.

Cops, Protests, Class War and Capitalism

June 2 and June 18, 2020
Wolff Responds

This is an interesting moment in American history, a turning point. If I can guess about the future, I believe it is a turning point because the injustices and inequalities that have accumulated over the last 40 years—and that go back much further into the depths of American history—have now finally produced the uprising that was always coming, but took a long time to arrive.

Capitalism has promised to bring great things to the human race. From its beginnings in the French Revolution, the people who wanted to end feudalism and bring in capitalism said it would bring liberty, equality, and fraternity. Americans, too, thought that revolting against British feudalism would bring similar change. As it says in the Declaration of Independence "life, liberty and the pursuit of happiness." They wanted to create a democratic system in which everybody who's affected by a decision has the right to participate equally in making it. Capitalism promised a lot.

However, on most of the really important things (liberty, equality, brotherhood, democracy) it didn't work out. The promises were broken. The goods were not delivered. We don't have equality, not when Jeffrey Bezos has $160 billion dollars while Los Angeles County in California announced last week that 66,000 people are living homeless on its streets, a 12% increase from the year before.

We are one of the richest countries in the world. We have a rich, developed medical establishment. We hear this frequently. Yet, here's a disturbing fact for you to struggle with: the United States has 5% of the world's population, but it has 25% of the world's deaths from the coronavirus. This is system failure.

We have incredible inequality in America today. Six hundred American billionaires together have more wealth than the bottom half of the population. A few people live in luxury while millions are denied enough money to feed their family, educate their children or furnish their home. People get bitter about this. They get envious about this. They get all the feelings you can imagine and understand.

What happens if a tiny number of people have enormous wealth and power while vast numbers of people don't? What happens when vast numbers of people have so little wealth and power that they're really living paycheck to paycheck, always on the edge, always worried, always in difficulty?

When you have a society divided in this way you need to enforce the peace.

A society broken apart in two extremes of rich and poor is a society riven with conflict. While the mass of people is worried about their poverty, the rich are worried about the fact that they're vulnerable because they're a minority. They're very small in number compared to the poor and the middle class and they're afraid that the majority will somehow take away what they have. The rich also direct their wealth at efforts to convince the rest of society, even those who don't have much, to be worried about any systemic change because perhaps even the little you do have will be taken from you too.

So, we're full of tension, suspicion, and trouble, into which we throw the police. Officers grow up in the same tension ridden society and when they join the police force, they discover that their job is to keep the lid on this exploding society. It's a tough world and poor and middle-income people are being constantly ripped off, but the police are supposed to contain and repress people who say "I don't want to be ripped off anymore. I want to be treated like a human being. I want to be given a reasonable share of the wealth I helped to create when I work." Cops thrown into that situation often don't act well.

The police are still composed of individuals with individual choice. They didn't have to take that job, and if they took it they didn't have to be mean, nasty, vicious. But I also want to stress (not by way of excusing anything but by way of understanding) that police are given a task no one can achieve. That's why their situation is absurd and dangerous. They go overboard and use excess force all the time.

Police can't solve the problem. That's why throwing them at it is cruel for the population they abuse, and cruel for the monsters those police must sooner or later become if they do not withdraw either from the police force or from the social role that is assigned to the police.

We are in the midst of a prolonged war, a class struggle in which the employer class (a small minority) wages war on the labor force (the hundred and sixty million Americans who produce the goods and services we all depend on). Those hundred and sixty million are under assault. They have been for decades. Their real wages, which is the money they earn compared to the prices they have to pay, have not gone up in 35 years.

They compensate for the loss of a rising income by having more members of the family go out to do more labor hours, and by borrowing more money than any working class in the history of the world.

By 2008, as we know, the combination of physical and mental exhaustion on the one hand and unsupportable, unsustainable debts on the other collapsed the capitalist economy. This economy had relied on exhausting workers and lending them the money that before had been paid to them as wages. It was impossible to keep up and the system folded. Capitalism as a system survived, as it usually has in the last 300 years. It figured out how to keep the system going without changing it, forcing people back into the very roles, the same inequality, and the same unsustainable debts that had led them into the crash.

By 2020, when confronted with one of the viruses that periodically plague the human race, an exhausted US capitalism fell apart in a matter of nine weeks. 40 million people were thrown out of work and forced to stay at home because of the virus. This puts the American working class under unbearable pressure. Would the job even be there after you come off of unemployment? Who knows! Will you get sick? Who knows! How will you cope with life under these uncertainties? Who knows! How am I ever going to pay my debts? Who knows! The working class has been subjected to something that's impossible to cope with.

Additionally, for the 120 million who still have a job, competition threatens them. Employers compete with one another, trying to lower the cost of production so they can lower their prices and beat their competitor. How are they going to lower the cost of production now? They're going to cut your wage and benefits. They're going to ask you to come in a half an hour earlier, leave a half an hour later and take a shorter lunch break. And if you say, "I won't tolerate it," the employer will say, "Fine. Go ahead and quit. I've got 40 million people getting more desperate each week to have some job, any job! They'll take the job at the now reduced arrangements I offered you." If you thought that the laboring working class in this country has been under pressure, that pressure is now being intensified.

How do the capitalists hope to survive this catastrophic crash, the worst since the 1929 economic collapse? Coupled with their failed management of the virus, they use the same old methods: divide the workers who are angry. Make the white ones angry at the black ones. Make the black ones angry at the white ones. Make the population furious at the cops and vice versa. Among those at the top, they're laughing all the way to their banks.

In 2019 alone, US police killed 1,004 people. Over the same year, police in England and Wales killed just three. Nine in Australia. Two in Japan. None in Denmark. You get the point. The US divides people and kills large numbers to keep a system in place that could not save us from a pandemic or an economic crash. Now the society is plunging into worse inequality than we already had.

Will US capitalism survive? Or will this be the time when white and black people understand that the system is the main problem, not each other? It will be hard. That's why it's worked so well to keep capitalism in place. But it's the system that's the key issue.

We will not solve the poverty problem and the racial problems of this country without a fundamental change in how people get jobs, incomes, homes, automobiles, vacations, university educations, you name it. That's the social change that ought to come out of the courageous people reminding us that black lives matter; that equality is something we can continue to fight for and that we need it because the alternative is a society no one will want to live in.

This system is over. It cannot support the society into which it was born, in which it grew, and changed. Now it must pass away to make room for a system that works better for most people than this one has shown it can.

This essay has been adapted from two "Wolff Responds" videos on Professor Wolff's YouTube channel: "Protests and Class War" posted on June 2 and "Cops and Capitalism" posted on June 18, 2020.

How Racism Is an Essential Tool for Maintaining the Capitalist Order

June 24, 2020
Independent Media Institute

U.S. capitalism survived because it found a solution to the basic problem of its instability, its business cycles. Since capitalism never could end cyclical downturns and their awful effects, its survival required making those effects somehow socially tolerable. Systemic racism survived in the post-Civil War United States partly because it helped to achieve that tolerability. Capitalism provided conditions for the reproduction of systemic racism, and vice versa.

Every four to seven years, on average, capitalism produces a downturn ("recession," "depression," "bust," "crash"—many words for a problem so regularly repeated). Political leaders, economists, and others have long searched for a cure for capitalism's instability. None was ever found. Capitalism has thus already recorded three crashes in this new century (spring of 2000, autumn of 2008, and now in 2020).

Defenders of capitalism prefer to call its inescapable instability the "business cycle." That sounds less awful. Yet its cycles' hard reality has always frightened capitalism's defenders. They recognize that when large numbers of people suddenly lose their jobs, many businesses die, production shrinks, and governments lose tax revenues, the results can and often do threaten the entire economic system. Capitalism's cyclical crises could potentially turn their victims against it and make them receptive to the system's critics.

This would more likely happen if everyone in the society were roughly equally vulnerable to cyclical downturns. Most employees would then rightly worry that their jobs would be lost in the next crash. They would periodically face income losses, interrupted educations, lost homes, and so on. Whatever relief employees felt if neighbors, rather than themselves, got fired, they would know that it might well be their turn in the next cycle. The losses, insecurities, and anxieties produced by such a capitalism would long ago have turned employees against it and provoked transition to a different system.

U.S. capitalism solved its instability problem by making cyclical downturns afflict chiefly a minority subpart of the whole working class. It positioned that minority to bear the brunt of each cycle and suffer its damages disproportionally. That minority was repeatedly drawn into and then thrown out of jobs as the cycle dictated. Any savings it might accumulate when working would be lost when unemployed. Repeated firings precluded such a minority from enjoying the benefits of job longevity (seniority, promotion, household stability, etc.). Poverty, disrupted households and families, unaffordable housing, education, and medical care would haunt such a minority. It would become capitalism's "business cycle shock-absorber"—the last hired, first fired—across the four-to-seven-year average duration of its cycles.

For capitalism, making such a minority absorb most of the costs of capitalism's instability allowed the majority of the working class to be relatively exempted, relieved, freed from them. The majority could be less subject to cycles because the minority was made relatively much more subject. Capitalism promised the majority relatively secure jobs and incomes because it took those away from the minority. The majority could thus worry less about the next cycle, whereas the minority had to worry more and adjust their lives more. Racists could then attribute the resulting differences between minority and majority subparts of a population to inherent qualities of different "races" instead.

Other advanced capitalist countries found parallel solutions. Some condemned immigrants to play the role assigned to African Americans in the United States. Racism aimed at immigrants often followed. In cyclical upswings, immigrants would be brought in: North Africans into France, southern Italians into Switzerland, Turks into Germany, and so on. Then, cyclical downswings would return those immigrants to their home countries. Capitalisms would thus save on costs of unemployment insurance, welfare payments, etc., for the workers who had returned. While some capitalisms relied on domestic minorities to be shock-absorbers and others relied on immigrants, some countries relied on both. The United States used Central American immigrants alongside domestic African Americans, and it still does. Germany allowed some immigrants to settle and acquire German citizenship alongside Turkish and other immigrant "guest workers."

In the United States, married white women also played the role of business cycle shock-absorber. During cyclical upswings, they would enter the paid labor force in part-time or full-time positions. Like African Americans, they earned less than white men. Women's jobs, too, were likely to be temporary, undone by cyclical downturns.

Whatever communities were forced into the shock-absorber role, poverty, depression, broken families, slums, and inadequate education and health facilities became more widespread among them than they were among the majority of the working class. Insecure jobs, incomes, homes, and lives often bred bitterness, envy, desperation, crime, and violence. These collateral damages had to be "managed" by the capitalisms whose survival depended on producing and reproducing those communities. Police and prisons were and are assigned that management task.

Police and prisons were to "keep the lid on," "tame," "patrol and control" the restive portions of the shock-absorber communities sequestered in slums or ghettos. Interactions with police coupled with cycling and recycling through prisons were the chosen means to manage capitalism's collateral damage. Those means generated collateral damage of their own: the long, tragic record of police violence, use of excessive force, the harshness and violence of incarceration, and the killing especially of African Americans.

Why were African Americans "chosen" to be key (but not the only) cyclical shock-absorbers in the United States? One factor concerned the racist legacies of U.S. slavery. They included beliefs that slaves were either not fully human or inferior humans. Even the U.S. Constitution had counted a slave as merely three-fifths of a full (i.e., white) person for census purposes. Accommodation to slavery before the U.S. Civil War had already shaped a racialized consciousness in both masters and slaves. And because U.S. slavery entailed different skin colors for masters and slaves (unlike many slaveries in world history), a readily identifiable minority had already been defined in racial terms in the slave portions of the United States. Moreover, that definition had spread to other parts of the United States as well. U.S. capitalism used, absorbed, and built on slavery's legacy by inserting large portions of the African American community into the shock-absorber role that the system required. The racism developed by U.S. slavery thereby both facilitated U.S. capitalism and was reinforced by it.

A significant portion of the white working class in all capitalisms has always also been forced into the shock-absorber role. "White trash" in U.S. capitalism was never far from the African Americans similarly situated. There thus arose possibilities of class solidarity between these Black and white working-class communities. U.S. history displays moments when those possibilities were realized, as C. Vann Woodward documented so well. It also displays moments of intense racist violence used to block the realization of those possibilities. Employers played on racialized differences to keep employees from unifying against them. In bitter competitions between Black and white shock-absorbers for cyclically scarce jobs, whites could and often did use racism to gain advantages in access to those jobs. In multiple ways, then, capitalism fostered and benefited from racism; it thus settled deeply into the system.

Fundamental injustice characterized the relationship between police and prisons, on the one hand, and the African American and other communities (Indigenous, people of color) condemned to play capitalism's shock-absorber role, on the other. The solution was and is not better training or more funding; both have been tried repeatedly and both have likewise failed repeatedly. A real solution would provide a decently paid job to everyone who wants one as a matter of right. Unemployment would then be outlawed much like slavery, child abuse, etc. Taxes levied on capitalist enterprises would provide the funds needed to find jobs, private or public, for those laid off by an employer (much as such taxes help fund unemployment insurance now). Those funds would include wages or salaries paid for each worker's time between being laid off and rehired. Minimum wages, applied universally, would cover reasonable housing, transport, health care and other living costs.

If such a solution were deemed to be incompatible with capitalism as a system, capitalism would have to give way to a system that made adequately paid employment a basic right for all. Enterprise profit would then finally be ejected from its throne as capitalism's number one social priority.

Such a solution would finally free African Americans, Indigenous, and Brown people from long-standing abuses in and by police and prisons. It would thus reduce the racism that those institutions have exemplified and reinforced. It would also reduce pressures on police and prison personnel to behave in ways that self-destructively rob them of their humanity as well as oppress others. Police and prisons in the United States today serve an inherently unstable capitalism by means of systemic racism. The logic of alliance between anti-racism and anti-capitalism could not be clearer.

This article was published and syndicated by the Independent Media Institute's Economy for All project on June 24, 2020.

Brick and mortar, crumbling: The COVID pandemic has cemented Amazon's dominant position. What now?

July 11, 2020
Op-ed, New York Daily News

"All the lonely people, where do they all come from?" So wondered the Beatles famously. Today's answer would be "from isolation in front of computers." In recent years, millions of customers have lost interest in and abandoned malls across America, not to mention more traditional brick-and-mortar storefronts that make cities like New York so vibrant.

Well before the coronavirus hit, many commercial strips had been reeling, and malls had been collapsing into bankruptcy by the thousands. Shoppers increasingly saved money and time by ordering from home via the internet and getting package deliveries; when they did venture out, it was often to big-box stores.

During the last few months, huge numbers of smaller stores have closed. Walmarts and Targets have been open and online shopping has become even more widespread, accelerating an Amazonification of America that had already been well underway. What we do about this will largely determine whether we still have functioning public commercial spaces in this country — or whether we fold up our tent and accept that relatively efficient and inexpensive delivery of goods straight to the home will dominate our retail economy for generations to come.

The answer matters mightily. Many have forgotten this, but markets are not just places where we go to get goods. They are a defining characteristic of civilization as we know it.

Once, isolated households were self-sufficient in most ways, each producing what it needed to survive. Then, a division of labor slowly evolved. People learned that when each household produced just one or a few products, a community of households could achieve a greater total output of goods and services.

That enabled higher standards of consumption and living. To achieve them, communities needed some institution — a council of elders, a chief, a religious or secular leader, etc. — to distribute each household's output to all the others who wanted to consume it. Sometimes that institution was a market, where goods and services were distributed by means of exchanges among producers and consumers.

Trips to markets became passages into community. Leaving isolation, at least temporarily, people in markets enjoyed interpersonal contacts and socialized activities. They found friends, lovers and partners, and came to discuss and act together to solve shared problems.

Their influence went far beyond this function. Villages, towns and cities grew up around markets. People overcame isolation not only by buying from one another. They also brought their workplaces and schools, as well as their homes, nearer to markets both to work and shop more easily and for all the social connections and interactions markets fostered.

Modern society has been shaped indispensably by markets and their evolution. It will be deeply affected if real markets mostly vanish, replaced by merely electronic, virtual forms.

We are now living through a remarkable moment in the history of markets, and therefore in the history of contemporary civilization. Countless shopping places inside malls and on cities' high streets keep disappearing. In their place, Amazon, Walmart and a very few other giants dominate, pleasing us with their prices and selection and efficiency but letting us down in so many other ways.

We are becoming siloed, isolated again in households, this time staring at computer screens and opening packages. Social indicators show that we are understandably lonely and becoming lonelier. This year's lockdown aiming to contain the pandemic has only intensified that process, putting mega-retailers who dominate the internet even more firmly in the catbird's seat.

Where do we go from here? Is there any way we can reestablish the centrality of common shopping spaces? If not, what will happen to our communities as we know them, and to our sense of ourselves?

The answer lies in an economic principle about competition within markets themselves. Typically, the producer able to charge the lowest price for a good or service in a market will "win" the competition among sellers to find buyers. That is because buyers will flock to that producer and abandon others, "losers" in the competition.

Winners grow and losers die. Winners often buy the losers' equipment and facilities and hire some of the losers' laid-off workers. In short, winners absorb losers. This repeats until one seller is left in each market. Competition destroys itself to become its opposite, monopoly.

Having no competition — nowhere else for buyers to go — monopolies can raise their prices far beyond their production costs and thereby realize monopoly profits.

But then the process switches into reverse. High monopoly profits lure other capitalists. They seek to enter monopolized markets. If and when they do, monopoly self-destructs to return to competition. And that competition, once returned, will eventually resume its evolution into monopoly.

In capitalism, therefore, competition and monopoly are opposites that produce one another as sequential market phases.

If we are lucky — if this basic economic narrative holds — internet behemoths and more authentic, close-to-home brick-and-mortar stores may exhibit a parallel sequence.

Internet sellers deliver a vast array of products at prices lower than what storekeepers can charge. What department stores had earlier done to small specialty stores, internet sellers have done to malls and other retailers. By attracting buyers, internet shopping is defeating brick-and-mortar stores; it is fast absorbing their equipment, physical space and some of their former employees.

There are other reasons for this. Because average U.S. wages have been stagnant for decades, price has become ever more important to buyers. Then the coronavirus pandemic made matters worse. As government bailouts allowed millions to become unemployed, they have focused even more on price. As government directives have urged them to stay at home, they have valued delivery even more.

When retail stores collapse, the wealth lost (in jobs, businesses, invested capital, and by surrounding communities dependent on them) far exceeds the added profits of the internet's major corporate sellers. Under capitalism's usual rules, those sellers have no obligation to compensate those who suffer on the other side.

So is the march of traditional retail to extinction inevitable? Or might this be another phase, one ultimately leading to another chapter, of monopoly and competition?

I think there's hope for retail as we have long known it, from mom-and-pop stores to franchises to malls. If they take the necessary steps, they can offer shoppers benefits that the internet cannot. The problem is not unsolvable, nor need we stand helplessly by as the logic of capitalism dictates painful switches back and forth from one shopping system to another. Policy can intervene to achieve a democratically decided choice of commercial opportunities for buyers as well as sellers.

Those steps begin with a basic recognition, one that we have long since forgotten: Buyers suffer a heavy non-monetary loss when they shift to internet shopping.

The key word to describe the loss is loneliness, long a growing problem in the U.S. We spend ever more time before screens on computers, smartphones and TVs. Shopping face-to-face has long been very different.

As has been known since at least Socrates' time, humans are social animals. People gather in groups to exist in nature, to reproduce and raise families, to enjoy goods and services that cannot be produced by isolated individuals but only by groups or collective efforts. Sports, dances, restaurants and most other entertainments require people to gather in groups. Escaping loneliness has always been a major part of what we enjoy about our activities with others.

Going to markets in malls, at county fairs, along Fifth Ave., and at tag sales overcomes loneliness.

We probably can't continue self-isolating forever. Likely sooner than later, Americans will react to their worsened loneliness. Venal politicians tap into this when they advocate "reopening America" despite serious viral risks. We ultimately want to venture out, and have contact with one another, for the same reasons that isolated farmers went on market day to gather with one another, that shy teenagers had reasons of their own to do likewise, that older people maintained lifelong friendships and started new ones.

The internet is far better for selling goods than selling services precisely because services are, by definition, more about interpersonal interactions. So traditional retail spaces need to focus more on services than goods and more on the service aspects of goods than on the goods themselves. Buying a service from another person is likewise getting it, and that is much less lonely than buying a good via the internet.

At the same time, our commercial centers need to become sites — made rigorously safe and healthy — for all manner of arts, crafts and other engaging spectacles. Many commercial strips already do this, but more need to follow their example.

Places need to be established in and around brick-and-mortar stores for political debates, speeches, organizing, all of which nourish us in ways we don't appreciate. Inside or adjacent sports facilities need to be readily available. Stalls for temporary stores need to be interspersed with permanent stores so as to maximize continuously new and different shopping possibilities.

Rather than letting our shopping strips and malls wither and die, we need to commit to making them rich, diverse, unique gathering places, places that ennoble and uplift and excite people in ways that big box stores and internet retail simply cannot, no matter how hard they try.

Of course, historic opportunities require collective planning and collective actions. Most leaders of U.S. fear such collective undertakings led by the only institutions capable of achieving them: local, regional and national governments. So they may fail to solve a major social problem in the U.S. It would not be the first time.

This article was published in the New York Daily News on July 11, 2020.

Profiting off the Suffering of Millions

July 8 and 18, 2020
Wolff Responds

I would like to address the stark level of injustice that is shocking even for me, and I watch these things more than I probably should. Over the last 15 or 16 weeks, over 52 million Americans filed for unemployment. They are using up their savings if they are lucky enough to have any, or leaning on relatives, friends, and communities for support. They are worried sick about whether their jobs will still be there when the economy picks back up and, if so, whether their salary and working conditions will be the same. Unfortunately, millions of those jobs have disappeared forever.

What a mess of suffering that could have been avoided. Kids don't learn, teachers can't teach, people who want to work can't, and millions of others are locked indoors.

But I want you to think about those who *can*, those who make a lot of money off the limits that hold us back. We permit in this society a vast injustice in which huge numbers of our fellow citizens suffer while a few cash in. I'm not talking about making honest profits, I'm talking about making record sums off the suffering of others. Let me give some examples to those of you that have morals and ethics (religious or not).

The United States Treasury has recently listed the companies that received money under the Paycheck Protection Program (PPP)[1], the relief fund that went into effect here in the United States to deal with the COVID-19 pandemic. Over half a trillion dollars ($521 billion to be exact) were dispersed under this program and recent media releases have indicated that well-connected people, friends of politicians, big businesses, supporters of Mr. Trump, and all sorts of everyday corruption were involved here, too.

JP Morgan Chase recently and proudly announced their record profits while most Americans suffered the pandemic and plus capitalism's crash. Amazon suddenly got a burst of business. The good part of that is at least some more people got jobs delivering what we can't go to the store to buy anymore. But then they've charged so much for the delivery that they not only get the extra money to pay the extra people, but they've beefed up their profits.

---

[1] In full disclosure, Democracy at Work received $28,700 from the PPP.

And they do it with a big smile, as if it's the American way to make a buck off the suffering of others. Isn't that the capitalist dream? Maybe. But as George Carlin once said, if you believe in the "American Dream," you need to know why it's called the American "dream:" you've got to be asleep to believe it.

UnitedHealth, a major national medical insurance company, recently reported record profits. That was bad enough. We have record unemployment, record suffering, a record number of people going to food banks, and UnitedHealth is making record profits?! My antennae went up. So I read the explanation of why profits were soaring that UnitedHealth provided to the press. It was something I was not prepared for.

It turns out that record numbers of Americans were terrified about the virus, understandably. So much so that, even when they felt unwell, they chose not to visit a doctor, clinic, or hospital. One reason was fear of being near people who had COVID-19. Another reason was the need to save money (on costly deductibles and copays) by postponing treatment or just waiting for the pain to pass. So millions who needed it did not get medical care.

For the insurance company, this was great news. They kept getting paid their usual premiums for health insurance but their payers feared to use it. Lower costs, higher profits, and one very happy insurer.

Folks, that's outrageous. That is neither necessary nor appropriate. This company could have been left with its usual profit, it might have even said that it didn't want extra when it is known to derive from people not getting health care, risking bigger health problems by postponing treatment. UnitedHealth could have understood that they have no right to get more profit out of the suffering of millions. But such thoughts seem scarce among CEOs of most capitalist corporations.

Profiteering off the misery of others is not something any decent society needs to permit.

The reason it occurs is the system. The PPP loans are a case in point. When the government gives money to a business, it does NOT give that money to everyone in the business. The government money goes to the people who run the business and that's not the same thing. Those who run the business are a tiny group of people at the top, the owner if it's a little company, or the Board of Directors of big corporations. The major shareholders of big corporations select the people on the board and therefore govern pretty much what they do. Owners and directors together are a tiny minority of all the people involved in the businesses. Most, of course, are employees.

So, government money is given to the tiny minority of folks at the top of recipient companies and that minority decides how to use it. No one knows exactly what the PPP money will be used for, because that is the purview of a private business run by that tiny minority. They might use it (if they cannot recover from the pandemic) in all kinds of ways that feather their nest and do nothing for the employees, who are left wondering whether their jobs will ever resume.

The irony is that the PPP is ultimately paid by the taxpayer. We all get to help pay for a program that gives money to a tiny minority who will decide how to use it and whether indeed in the longer run our paychecks will be protected. Yet we're all going through the pandemic together, or so we've been told.

The corruption does not lie in the people who are connected, snatching more than they ought to. Of course that goes on, but that's based in our system. The much deeper and much more pervasive corruption is allowing the existence of such a system, one that allows a tiny minority of people at the top to make all the decisions, governing who has a job, how much money they earn, the conditions of their job, the security of their job. Meanwhile, the mass of people is passive. We don't live under a real democracy, nor have we ever.

How different it would be if each person working in each enterprise had an equal vote about what to do with the government money intended to help us all. We could decide in a truly democratic manner how best to get that enterprise through the pandemic and the crash. The system is the problem. Until we change the system, we will see this kind of corruption surface and persist throughout our lifetimes and those of our children.

This essay has been adapted from two "Wolff Responds" videos on Professor Wolff's YouTube channel: "The Deep Corruption of Gov't Stimulus Programs" posted on July 8 and "Corporations Profit from Peoples' Suffering" posted on 18, 2020.

The Consequences of Inequality Can Be Fatal

July 30, 2020
Independent Media Institute

Capitalism, as Thomas Piketty's *Capital in the Twenty-First Century* shows, relentlessly worsens wealth and income inequalities. That inherent tendency is only occasionally stopped or reversed when masses of people rise up against it. That happened, for example, in western Europe and the U.S. during the 1930s Great Depression. It prompted social democracy in Europe and the New Deal in the United States. So far in capitalism's history, however, stoppages or reversals around the world proved temporary. The last half-century witnessed a neoliberal reaction that rolled back both European social democracy and the New Deal. Capitalism has always managed to resume its tendential movement toward greater inequality.

Among the consequences of a system with such a tendency, many are awful. We are living through one now as the COVID-19 pandemic, inadequately contained by the U.S. system, savages Americans of middle and lower incomes and wealth markedly more than the rich. The rich buy better health care and diets, second homes away from crowded cities, better connections to get government bailouts, and so on. Many of the poor are homeless. Tasteless advice to "shelter at home" is, for them, absurd. Low-income people are often crowded into the kinds of dense housing and dense working conditions that facilitate infection. Poor residents of low-cost nursing homes die disproportionally, as do prison inmates (mostly poor). Pandemic capitalism distributes death in inverse proportion to wealth and income.

Social distancing has destroyed especially low-wage service sector jobs. Rarely did top executives lose their positions, and when they did, they found others. The result is a widened gap between high salaries for some and low or no wages for many. Unemployment invites employers to lower wages for the still employed because they can. Pandemic capitalism has provoked a massive increase in money-creation by central banks. That money fuels rising stock markets and thereby enriches the rich who own most shares. The coincidence of rising stock markets and mass unemployment plus falling wages only adds momentum to worsening inequality.

Unequal economic distributions (of income and wealth) finance unequal political outcomes. Whenever a small minority enjoys concentrated wealth within a society committed to universal suffrage, the rich quickly understand their vulnerability. The non-wealthy majority can use universal suffrage to prevail politically. The majority's political power could then undo the results of the economy including its unequal distribution of income and wealth. The rich corrupt politics with their money to prevent exactly that outcome. Capitalists spend part of their wealth to preserve (and enlarge) all of their wealth.

The rich and those eager to join them in the U.S. dominate within both Republican and Democratic parties. The rich provide most of the donations that sustain candidates and parties, the funding for armies of lobbyists "advising" legislators, the bribes, and many issue-oriented public campaigns. The laws and regulations that flow from Washington, states, and cities reflect the needs and desires of the rich far more than those of the rest of us. The peculiar structure of U.S. property taxes offers an example. In the U.S., property is divided into two kinds: tangible and intangible. Tangible property includes land, buildings, business inventories, automobiles, etc. Intangible property is mostly stocks and bonds. Rich people hold most of their wealth in the form of intangible property. It is thus remarkable that in the U.S., only tangible property is subject to property tax. Intangible property is not subject to any property tax.

The kinds of property (tangible) that many people own get taxed, but the kinds of property (intangible) mostly owned by the richest minority do not get taxed. If you own a house rented to tenants, you pay a property tax to the municipality where the house is located. You also pay an income tax on the received rents to the federal government and likely also the state government where you live. You are thus taxed twice: once on the value of the property you own and once on the income you derive from that property. If you sell a $100,000 house and then buy $100,000 worth of shares, you will owe no property taxes to any level of government in the United States. You will only owe income tax on dividends paid to you on the shares you own. The form of property you own determines whether you pay property tax or not.

This property tax system is excellent for those rich enough to buy significant amounts of shares. The rich used their wealth to get tax laws written that way for them. The rest of us pay more in taxes because the rich pay less. Because the rich save money—since their intangible property is not taxed—they have that much more to buy the politicians who secure such a tax system for them. And that tax system worsens inequality of wealth and income.

Unequal economic distributions finance unequal cultural outcomes. For example, the goal of a unifying, democratizing public school system has always been subverted by economic inequality. In general (with few exceptions), the better schools cost more to attend. The tutors needed to help struggling students are affordable for the rich but less so for everyone else. The children of the wealthy get the private schools, books, quiet rooms, computers, educational trips, extra art and music lessons, and virtually everything else needed for higher educational achievement.

Unequal economic distributions finance unequal "natural" outcomes. The U.S. now displays two differently priced foods. Rich people can afford "organic" while the rest of us worry but still buy "conventional" food for budget reasons. Countless studies indicate the dangers of herbicides, pesticides, chemical fertilizers, food processing methods, and additives. Nonetheless, the two-price food system delivers the better, safer food more to the rich than to everyone else. Likewise, the rich buy the safer automobiles, more safely equip their homes, and clean and filter the water they drink and the air they breathe. No wonder the rich live years longer on average than other people. Inequality is often fatal, not just during pandemics.

In ancient Greece, Plato and Aristotle worried about and discussed the threat to community, to social cohesion, posed by inequalities of wealth and income. They criticized markets as institutions because, in their view, markets facilitated and aggravated income and wealth inequalities. But modern capitalism sanctifies markets and has thus conveniently forgotten Plato's and Aristotle's cautions and warnings about markets and inequality.

The thousands of years since Plato and Aristotle have seen countless critiques, reforms, and revolutions directed against wealth and income inequalities. They have rarely succeeded and have even more rarely persisted. Pessimists have responded, as the Bible does, with the notion that "the poor shall always be with us." We rather ask the question: Why did so many heroic efforts at equality fail?

The answer concerns the economic system, and how it organizes the people who work to produce and distribute the goods and services societies depend on. If its economic organization splits participants into a small rich minority and a large non-rich majority, the former will likely be determined to reproduce that organization over time. Slavery (master versus slave) did; feudalism (lord versus serf) did; and capitalism (employer versus employee) does. Inequality in the economy is a root cause contributing to society-wide inequalities.

We might then infer that an alternative economic system based on a democratically organized community producing goods and services—not split into a dominant minority and a subordinate majority—might finally end social inequality.

This article was published and syndicated by the Independent Media Institute's Economy for All project on July 30, 2020.

Part IV

Capitalism and Reform:
Resist, Evade, Weaken, Repeal

Capitalism Is the Reason Your Employer Is Screwing You Over

June 15, 2018
Huffington Post

Few businesses show the skewed dynamics between employer and employees as clearly as Amazon. Its CEO Jeff Bezos is the world's richest person, with his wealth estimated at around $130 billion. He admits the near impossibility of spending these riches and commits $1 billion a year of his "Amazon winnings" to fund a personal project of space travel.

Back on Earth, Amazon's 560,000 employees earn a median salary of $28,000, its warehouse workers face strict efficiency targets that lead some to relieve themselves in trash cans, and hundreds of Ohio, Arizona and Pennsylvania-based workers are on food stamps.

To understand why the relationship between employer and employee is so severely screwed, we have to look to capitalism.

Capitalist businesses are starkly undemocratic. Employers are economic dictators. They wield enormous power and control that is unaccountable to the social majority around them: their employees and the communities in which they live.

Employees' labor produces profits, which belong 100 percent to the employers. Yet workers are excluded from decisions about how to use those profits. Instead, they depend on wages (set and controlled by the employer) as compensation for the work they produce.

Employers' decisions shape major aspects of employees' lives, both at work and away from it. The employer alone decides which commodities to produce, what production technology to use (with what side effects), where to locate the workplace, as well as what to do with the profits. Celebrations of employers' risks, used to justify their profits, rarely even recognize that workers, too, take risks in their dependence on employers (but without getting profits for doing so).

The skills employees develop, the personal connections they make, the seniority they accumulate, the home they invest in, their personal connections (in neighborhoods, schools, churches, etc.) — always risk being lost or diminished by decisions exclusively in employers' hands. Above all is the decision to end a worker's job.

While an employee deciding to leave a business will likely make little or no impact on an employer; employers' decisions to, for example, relocate production overseas, or sell or close a business, carry huge risks for employees.

This undemocratic organization of production increasingly concentrates income and wealth, as well as economic power, in a tiny percentage of the population.

Those concentrations dominate politics as well. Fundraising for political campaigns and policies tends to rely on those with the most resources to offer. Wealth translates into political influence. The result is a system of decisions that protect and strengthen capitalism.

In the realm of culture, the ideas of the top 1 percent — overwhelmingly capitalists — usually become the ruling ideas of the culture's arts, religions, media, and so on.

There is an answer — a mechanism that can bring democracy into the workplace: worker cooperatives. Under the cooperative model, workers have decision-making power that corresponds to the risks and productivity of their employment. Each worker gets an equal vote on decisions, which are made on a majority basis.

All share democratically in the company's gains and losses. If mistakes are made that threaten, weaken or even destroy the enterprise, those mistakes will flow from the affected workers' democratic decisions.

Some capitalist economies have already made concessions to workers demanding more than undemocratic dependency. Halfway measures, such as the German concept of *Mitbestimmung,* or co-determination, for example, allow workers to participate in the management of a company.

Workers have also sometimes gained ownership of parts or even all of the enterprises where they work (for example, employee stock ownership plans in the U.S.). But worker ownership alone is fundamentally insufficient. In most capitalist economies, such measures still exclude workers from the actual direction and control of enterprises.

Worker co-ops put the workers in direct control. They democratize the direction of companies, rather than just giving employees a stake in some of the management decisions. Workers decide democratically who to hire and fire as managers, and direct their management activities. They become, in effect, their own board of directors.

In capitalism, benefits of improvements, for example in technology, flow mostly or only to one level: to directors, who are almost never workers as well. So, there is little incentive for workers to look for or make improvements in the efficiency of production. The same cannot be said of workers in co-ops, who have the dual roles of workers and directors.

Similarly, faced with opportunities for changes that increase profits but have negative environmental side effects, capitalist directors will more likely adopt them because they usually get the profits and can escape the side effects. Employees of those directors, who must bear the costs of the side effects for themselves, their families and neighbors, will give greater weight to the negative side effects versus the positive profits.

Worker co-ops also move away from huge pay disparity between those at the top and those at the bottom. All workers democratically decide on wages and bonuses, making it unlikely that they would give huge salary packages to only a very few.

Likewise, there are differences when it comes to the distribution of any profits or surpluses. Nothing plays a greater role in the dichotomy of 1 percent versus 99 percent than the undemocratic nature of capitalist decisions about how to distribute profits or surpluses.

Capitalist employers often distribute them as top executives' salary and stock option packages, dividend payouts, buying back their company's shares, and so on. Worker cooperatives take a democratic approach. They also typically decide how much goes to, for example, advertising, research and development, politicians, artists and civic contributions. Society is shaped in countless ways by corporate decisions about how profits are distributed.

However, in worker co-ops, the decision-making structure on distributing profits is an effective mechanism to reduce poverty, and income and wealth inequalities. They can, for example, devote surpluses to providing workers or area residents with social services, instead of paying dividends or advertising. Their goals in providing funds to politicians would differ, as would their contributions to cultural groups.

For people to ever get a real choice about capitalist businesses versus worker co-ops — about what balance between them the economy should offer — there would have to be a worker-co-op sector of the U.S economy within easy reach of all Americans.

However, the U.S. economy is skewed by a government that has provided a vast array of services, tax advantages, and subsidies to capitalist businesses, with nothing remotely comparable for worker co-op businesses.

Sen. Kirsten Gillibrand (D-N.Y.) recently introduced legislation that would begin to rectify some of the anti-worker and anti-co-op discrimination in U.S. government policy by offering to help small businesses convert to co-ops and gain access to capital. Similarly, the Labour Party in the U.K. is on record with a commitment to establish a major worker co-op sector of the U.K. economy if it is elected.

If such a worker co-op sector were established economy-wide, we all could vote — with ballots and our wallets — for whatever mix of alternative enterprises we prefer. Concrete knowledge, as well as ideological commitments, could inform democratic choices about what mix of capitalist and worker co-op enterprises best suit us. And if Republicans and Democrats are too dependent on capitalists' contributions, perhaps we need an independent political movement or a party to advocate for building such a worker co-op segment of the economy.

This article was published in the Huffington Post on June 15, 2018.

Pandemic Response Reflects the Priorities of US Capitalism

April 3, 2020
Wolff Responds

What is being done by the federal government in the United States is too little, too late, fundamentally ineffective, and unfair. If that's a harsh criticism, that's what it ought to be. The Fed has been pumping money into the system, but it hasn't solved the problems – neither the pandemic nor the economic meltdown. The Fed has also been cutting interest rates down to next to nothing, but that hasn't proved to be a solution either.

With the failure of monetary policy to really fix, let alone prevent, the economic collapse, we now see a turn to fiscal policy: the US Treasury, Republicans, Democrats, and president passing a bill in excess of $2 trillion to stimulate the economy. That is also too little and too late.

In the 1930s – the last time we had a depression as serious as the one we are now entering – President Roosevelt was under pressure from the unions, the CIO, two socialist parties, and a communist party, all of which were achieving record memberships at that time. Under that pressure, what did President Roosevelt do? Did he give everybody a check for $1,200, like the latest bill? No. He created Social Security, which we had never had before, and which gave every person 65 years of age or older a check every month for the rest of their lives. But that wasn't the only thing he did.

He also created the unemployment compensation system, which the US had never had. If you lost your job through no fault of your own, you got a weekly check for a year or two. Then Roosevelt went further and created a minimum-wage law. The purpose of the law was to limit employers' ability to cut workers' wages by threatening them with "If you don't like it, leave. Lots of unemployed people would grab that job at half what I pay you."

Roosevelt announced that if the private sector of the US economy either could not or would not hire the millions of Americans who only asked for a job, then he, as president, would. Between 1934 and 1941, he created and filled 15 million jobs. For these very expensive programs, the US government had little money (as masses of unemployed and bankrupt businesses paid no taxes). But it spent massively anyway, helping middle-income and poor people, not just big banks, corporations, and the rich. FDR practiced trickle-up as well as trickle-down economics. He had to because of the organized political pressure from below.

127

Now compare that to the small-minded reasoning and small amounts of money in Congress's recent stimulus bill. A one-shot deal of $1,200 and $500 per child? You must be kidding. That's an insult to our intelligence and our history. It is woefully inadequate to the scale of our problems – like so much this government and this private capitalist system have done.

Throwing money at this crisis, as this government is doing, will not solve it because it's not simply a money problem. It's an organizational problem. We have to reorganize the economy. We can't do business the way we did; it's too dangerous. When there has to be six or more feet between people and intensive cleaning and repeated testing, that requires a physical reorganization of how we do business.

As a professor, I think about how we teach. We have tens of millions of students – little babies; daycare kids; kids in elementary school, secondary school, college, and university. It's dangerous to meet in class, and the schools are all shut. But here's what we should have done, here's what we should have planned for, here's what we should be doing now: You switch from a classroom teaching structure to a tutorial structure. This is a well-known tactic. With one teacher, one student, you can be six or ten feet apart, in a safe space, one or two hours a day. Take millions of the unemployed and put them to work. Each of them knows something and can teach it – whatever he or she knows – whether it's typing, or singing, or making something in the woodshop. It doesn't matter. We could organize a one-on-one, safe environment, and we should. Learning can continue even if we have a pandemic.

But to do reorganization like this you have to reorganize, physically, how the economy works. Businesses aren't doing it – at all in most cases, or way too individually. Thus, progress is partial and slow. We need a massive program – the kind that can only be administered by the government. We don't have any other agency to do it.

But here's why we don't have that: because we live in a society that has always given priority to a special-interest-group minority called employers. They don't want the government to come in and reorganize their business because we might find that we don't ever want to go back. We want business to be done efficiently, for the society as a whole, and equipped to cope with emergencies like a pandemic. We don't want the private enterprise that just failed to prepare us for this virus failing now to cope with it. We want a different system. We want the workers in each workplace to run it so it's safe for them, the majority. And the capitalists, the employers, they know this. They don't want the solution because for them, like Mr. Trump said, for them it's worse than the disease.

Last point that you might be surprised to hear me say: Mr. Trump was recently very wise. He said, I don't want to shut the economy down. Remember, he was talking about how we'll all be packed in church on Easter; we will all be going back to work and shop. And Americans were shocked. And when they were shocked, Mr. Trump – here comes his wisdom – said to us, well, we didn't shut down the automobile factories just because we have tens of thousands of people killed in auto accidents every year. And that's wisdom. He's absolutely right. We don't shut down our private automobile system, despite the fact that it kills 50,000-60,000 of us every year.

But of course we should have. Long ago we should have had a system of efficient, rapid, frequent buses, jitneys, street railways, regular railways. We should have an adequate, clean, attractive public transportation system. It would pollute the air less, it would kill virtually none of us, it would not waste vast amounts of raw materials. That's much more efficient. And the only reason we haven't had it is because the private capitalist system can't cope with losing the profits from private automobiles.

Trump was right: It's just like the current situation. They want the pandemic to run its course. Half a million of us die, sort of like the car accident. This is what happens when capitalism reaches its end, when private profit literally trumps the public's health.

This essay has been adapted from "Wolff Responds: The Economics of The Coronavirus" posted on Professor Wolff's YouTube channel on April 3, 2020.

Fix Capitalism (yet again) or Do Better?

April 26, 2020
Independent Media Institute

Consider this absurdity: The U.S. government's policy in the face of the current capitalist crash is to "return the economy to the pre-coronavirus normal." What? In that "normal" system, private capitalists maximized profits by not producing the tests, masks, ventilators, beds, etc., needed when coronavirus hit. Profit-driven capitalism proved extremely inefficient in its response to the virus. Wealth already lost from the coronavirus far exceeds what it would have cost to prepare properly. In capitalism, a small minority—employers—makes all the key decisions (what, how, where to produce and how to use the proceeds) governing production and distribution of most goods and services. The majority—employees and their families—must live with the results of employers' decisions but are excluded from making them. Why return to such an undemocratic "normal"? Why fix capitalism yet again, given its structural disposition to cyclical crashes and repeated costly need to be fixed?

Look at this absurdity from another angle. When capitalist corporations fail, they often resort to declaring bankruptcy. That often means a court removes an existing leadership and turns the enterprise over to a different leadership team. Outside of legal bankruptcy, a failing capitalist enterprise may often experience its shareholders voting to oust one leadership team—one board of directors—and replacing it with another. While such steps recognize that capitalists do fail (and quite regularly), the solution they made into law changes only who are the employers. Bankruptcy neither questions nor changes the capitalist structure of the enterprise. But why maintain such a capitalist "normal?" Maybe the problem is the structure and not the particular executive team running the capitalist enterprise.

A staggering 20 million U.S. employees have lost their jobs and filed for unemployment benefits during the month before April 15. This is absurd. We the people, the public, will now pay a portion of the wages and salaries their employers no longer do. The unemployed will often blame themselves; many will lose connections to their skills, their former employer, and their fellow workers; many will worry about getting old jobs back; many will borrow (often too much); all will worry about mounting debts; etc. They would be far better off if they all got socially useful jobs as well as most of their former paychecks. The government could be such an employer of last resort: when private capitalists either cannot or will not hire because to do so is not profitable for them.

But capitalists almost always oppose public jobs. They fear the competition with private capitalists that state employment might entail. They worry that public employees will keep those jobs and not move back to private employment. To placate private capitalists, governments "fix" recessions and depressions—periods when capitalists fire workers—by sustaining the unemployed with cash for a while. Society loses as the public pays the workers' wages and salaries but gets no production of public goods and services in return.

Congress's recently passed law (CARES) plans to stimulate a crashed U.S. capitalism by giving major airlines some $25 billion to pay most of the wages and salaries of roughly 700,000 airline employees for the next six months. This is capitalist absurdity squared. Most of those employees will collect their paychecks but do no airline work because flying will remain too risky for too many over the next six months. One might expect airline employees to be required to do some sort of public service in return for their government paycheck. They might prepare safe workplaces to then produce the tests, masks, ventilators, gloves, etc., needed these days. They might be trained to test; to clean and disinfect workplaces, stores and athletic arenas; to teach using one-on-one social media tutorials; and so on. But no, in capitalist countries (with rare exceptions), private capitalists do not want and thus governments do not pass laws mandating that public sector jobs be required of the unemployed in exchange for their pay. Society loses, but capitalists are mollified.

Then, too, Boeing is getting a big bailout. That corporate leadership recently proved itself responsible for selling unsafe airplanes that killed hundreds, trying to hide its failures, and squeezing billions in public subsidies out of the state of Washington. Yet the government's bailout leaves Boeing leaders (and other employers getting government bailouts) in their traditional positions of making all key enterprise decisions exclusively and privately.

Why "fix" capitalism in these ways? Why the irrationality of unemployment pay without socially useful work for the unemployed? Why reproduce a normal capitalism that so undemocratically organizes its enterprises— where an unaccountable employer minority dictates to an employee majority? Why replace one group of employer dictators with another, when a better alternative presents itself? In short, why reproduce the capitalist (i.e., employer-employee) system generating socially divisive levels of unequal income and wealth almost everywhere plus business cycles regularly intruding instability?

Are we experiencing capitalism's historic decline? Is that the message as people increasingly find capitalism to be unnecessary at best and unbearable at worst? Worker cooperatives present themselves as a better alternative way to organize enterprises: factories, offices, and stores, private and public. As democratic economic institutions, worker coops are a better fit with and a much better support for democratic political institutions. For the 21st century, the most popular slogan on socialists' banners will likely be "Democratize the Enterprise."

In the 14th century, bubonic plague—the "Black Death"—exposed Europe's feudalism as vastly underfed, exhausted, dispirited, divided, and diseased. The infecting fleas carried by the rats could thus kill off a third of a very vulnerable continent. European feudalism never recovered its pre-bubonic strengths; its peak was behind it. Renaissance, reformation, and then the great English, French and American revolutions followed. The system collapsed amid transition to a new and different system, capitalism. Might the interactions now among capitalism, coronavirus, and a new worker-coop-based socialism prove similar to those among feudalism, the Black Death and capitalism so long ago?

This article was published and syndicated by the Independent Media Institute's Economy for All project on June 24, 2020.

The Meaning of a Booming Stock Market During a Pandemic

May 18, 2020
Wolff Responds

How is it possible, in the midst of the worst decline in our economy and worst levels of unemployment in a century, that the stock market is going up? This is a perfectly good question. The answer follows from the connection between the stock market and what goes on in the rest of the real world we live in.

There is some connection. Often, if stocks' prices are going up, their owners feel more comfortable about spending money and that shows up in more goods and services produced and sold. Likewise, when stock prices drop, owners usually spend less. When Main Street booms (production and employment rise) it often lifts share prices on Wall Street.

However, sometimes Main Street and Wall Street are very disconnected and go in opposite directions. Now is one of those times. The vast majority of Americans have no significant interest in the stock market. They either own no shares, or they own a quantity of shares in a pension fund that is managed by a big company, a big bank, etc. Maybe they have a few shares but not enough to make much of a difference. They care about production and jobs on the Main Streets of the country.

A different and much smaller group of people are concerned with Wall Street. Most corporations are run by a few 'major shareholders', the owners of big blocks of shares. Those include the very big banks, very wealthy individuals, insurance companies, large money managers, hedge funds, etc. They focus on share prices in stock markets. They do well when those prices are rising and poorly when they fall. When capitalism crashes, on average every 4-7 years, these people want the government to pump money into the economy with the hope and expectation that doing so will push up share prices.

In US capitalism's deep 2020 crisis, the Fed has been pumping massive amounts of money into the economy, much more than the large sums it pumped in during the last crisis in 2008-2009. That money goes first and foremost to big banks, but it now also goes to big corporations beyond the banks. Those big institutions, among the richest in our country, might take all of that extra money and trickle it down so it provides some sort of stimulus to the underlying economy. That might then stimulate producing

133

more goods and services by hiring more workers. That might mean good news for Main Street. The key word here is "might."

What should come as no surprise to most of you is an awful lot of the Fed's newly pumped in money never trickles very far down. Where does it go? Into the stock market.

The rich, the big banks, the insurance and money management companies: those are the main players on the stock market. As they get tons and tons of new government money, they lose the incentive to plow it into the Main Street economy. The millions of unemployed are not buying as they did before. Businesses in huge numbers have closed. There's no profit to be made in producing goods and services which your population in crisis cannot anymore afford. So, they put it into the stock market with the hope that they can buy the shares today and sell them two weeks, two months, two years from now at a higher price. The profit opportunities in the stock market are big and the profit opportunities in much of the rest of the economy are poorer.

So it should come as no surprise that the poor quality of our lives, our jobs, and our prospects on the one hand and the government pumping money into the economy on the other should end up with that money going to fuel an inflation of stock prices. It is a fun game for people who are in that business to buy and resell at a higher price, giving the stock market that peculiar quality of apparently booming when the rest of us are going in the opposite direction.

Is it a crazy arrangement? Absolutely. Is it fiercely unfair? You bet. But that's how capitalism works. If you don't want those injustices, if you don't want the people who are richest to be having a good time with public money while the rest of us are poor observers, then your problem is with capitalism, not with one or another of the details. This system works for the few at the top. It always has, and it's doing it now, despite a health crisis, despite an economic crash, as much as it ever did.

This essay has been adapted from "Wolff Responds: Today's Booming Stock Market" which was posted on Professor Wolff's YouTube channel on May 18, 2020.

Mass Unemployment Amid the Pandemic Is an Indictment of Capitalism

May 6, 2020
Truthout

Today's headlines scream at us about the trauma, pain and loss from an historic explosion of capitalist unemployment. Unemployment always stood as a mocking indictment of capitalism. Unemployment also threatens capitalism. This system rewards employers with profits from the waged labor of employees. Yet it fails to keep them working and thereby undermines its profits. Worse, that failure recurs quite regularly — a phenomenon known as the business cycle.

Its cycles expose capitalism as intrinsically socially irrational. Unemployed workers continue to consume, albeit in reduced quantities. They just stop producing. It would obviously be better to keep workers producing what they keep consuming. Capitalism cannot do that during its recurring cycles despite countless efforts, including Keynesian economics and policies since the 1930s. The cycles repeatedly cause much suffering and loss.

Still another irrationality of capitalism resides in most capitalists' obstinate refusal to consider, let alone implement, an obvious alternative to unemployment. When workers start being fired (because of falling demand, automation, etc.), employers could instead maintain employment but reduce workers' hours per week. Instead of 10 percent unemployment, cut the basic work week for all from 40 to 36 hours. All workers go home at 1 pm, not 5 pm, each Friday.

The costs of unemployment versus reduced hours are difficult to measure and thus compare. What likely explains most capitalists' preferences for unemployment is the power it allows them to wield over workers. The real prospect of unemployment keeps workers anxious, competing with one another to avoid eventually being the one fired. In this case, what is rational for the employers (a social minority) prevails despite it being irrational for employees (the majority). Even in a pandemic like today's, wherever social distancing can secure safe workplaces, substituting reduced hours for unemployment makes sense but remains rare.

The prospect of unemployment plagues workers and their families with anxieties. The experience of unemployment is associated with rising levels of depression, alcoholism, drug abuse, marital problems, child abuse, and other social ills. It is likewise associated with declining levels of worker self-esteem, job skills, personal savings, and physical and mental health.

Unemployment is unwanted by both employees and employers, yet it hits them again and again. Defenders of capitalism always worry: unemployed workers, as victims of capitalism, provide receptive audiences for its critics. Alliances of capitalism's victims and critics have challenged the system in the past and threaten it now again.

Unemployment is often part of a vicious cycle in capitalism. Unemployed workers lose incomes and therefore cut their consumption. That deprives capitalists producing workers' consumption commodities of market demand, sales, and thus profits. In response, those capitalists fire portions of their workforce. That worsens unemployment: the vicious cycle.

Many phenomena can trigger unemployment in capitalism. Whether each initial instance of unemployment descends into a vicious downward spiral depends on conditions within capitalism being triggered. For example, suppose changing consumer tastes mean less of commodity A gets purchased, and capitalists fire workers producing A. This might lead to a vicious downward cycle — but not if, for example, consumers shifted to buy more of commodity B. Capitalists might then hire the workers fired from A to take jobs making B.

The staggering, fast-rising unemployment spawned by capitalism's failures to prepare for and cope with the COVID-19 pandemic is different from our example. It has already set off a vicious downward spiral. The virus was the trigger, but a weakened capitalism reacted to the trigger with an economic crash. In the U.S. especially, much too little was done too late to counter — by increased employment elsewhere in the system — the unemployment set off by the pandemic. Increased hiring by delivery services, for example, fell far short of absorbing the millions fired from restaurants, bars, department stores, hotels, airlines, and so on. So, the downward spiral exploded.

None of this was necessary. As in the 1930s New Deal, the U.S. government could have undertaken a massive federal jobs program. That could have re-employed millions fired by employers who shut down the private sector. The list of socially useful tasks for such federal job holders includes campaigns across the U.S. for massive social coronavirus testing; for regular cleaning/disinfection of public spaces; for reorganizing public facilities to maintain social distancing when needed; for ongoing tutorials via social media for public school students (but also for the general public seeking to learn new skills); for "greening" the economy; for establishing a worker-cooperative sector of the economy, and so on.

Capitalism sees itself as a "rational" economic system. Yet, it is irrational to deprive employees of jobs when the tools, equipment and raw materials needed to produce socially useful goods and services are available. It is likewise irrational to allow workplaces to sit idle gathering rust and dust rather than reconfiguring or restructuring them to be safe as locations for socially useful production. It is irrational to undercut the needs of unemployed millions for the mental and physical health associated with meaningful labor. Last but not least, it is irrational to deprive the whole society of the goods and services capable of being produced by re-employed workers. If the private capitalist sector either cannot or will not re-employ in the socially most useful manner, then the government can and must do so.

If profit considerations lead private capitalists to decisions that are socially irrational — like firing millions of employees — then profit should not be society's decisive criterion. We should replace the profit system with different criteria, different "bottom lines" driving enterprise decisions. Such a system might usefully combine private and public enterprises organized, in both cases, as worker cooperatives. In them, workers make enterprise decisions democratically: Each worker gets an equal vote. Moreover, two other stakeholder groups participate, equally democratically, in reaching those decisions: (1) the consumers of each enterprise's output; and (2) the residents of the communities in which each enterprise functions.

Such a system would target the qualities and security of jobs, consumption and residence as key goals — "bottom lines" alongside enterprise profitability.

Proposing worker co-ops as frameworks for re-employing the millions deprived of work in capitalist crashes has a particular objective. Workers in worker co-op enterprises would much sooner see and act on unemployment's basic irrationality than capitalists typically do. The Italian region of Emilia-Romagna provides a useful example of a region where worker co-ops are institutionalized and comprise 40 percent of the economy. Its large co-op sector is a major contributor to the region's low unemployment rates (lower than Italy and also lower than the EU), its higher productivity rates, its outstanding GDP figures, and so on. Building such a sector in the United States would enable its residents to genuinely choose economic systems. Citizens could observe, purchase from, and work within enterprises organized as worker co-ops and thus compare them to their capitalistically organized counterparts. Then informed, democratic choices could be made as to what mix of the two alternative economic systems are wanted by the U.S. population.

Moving in such directions would go a long way toward finding and building on positive possibilities now buried under the catastrophic pile-up of a viral pandemic and a major capitalist crash.

This article was published in Truthout on May 6, 2020.

Capitalism vs Safety, Health: An Old Story Again

May 18, 2020
Independent Media Institute

A US President recently ordered meatpacking employees back into workplaces plagued by Coronavirus. He did NOT order the employers to make their slaughter houses safe. GOP-proposed legislation exempts employers from lawsuits by employees sickened or killed by coronavirus infections at workplaces. The GOP is mostly silent about requiring employers to maintain safe or healthy workplaces. Employers across the country threaten workers who refuse to return to jobs they find unsafe. They demand that employees return or risk being fired. Job loss likely means loss of health insurance for their families. Being fired risks also losing eligibility for unemployment insurance.

Employers are now going to extremes to evade the costs of safe and healthy workplaces. Recently, New Orleans' authorities and their contractors fired their $10.25 per hour garbage collectors after a short strike. The strikers had demanded protective equipment against garbage possibly infected with Corona and also $15 per hour "hazard" pay. New Orleans replaced the striking workers by contracting for nearby prison inmates paid $1.33 per hour and individuals from half-way houses. Capitalism's iron fist hits the working class with this "choice": unsafe job or poverty or slave labor with both.

Capitalism has always struggled to minimize outlays on workplace safety and health. Workers have protested this wherever capitalism became the prevailing economic system over the last 3 centuries. Upton Sinclair's popular book, The Jungle, published over a century ago, exposed spectacularly unsafe and unhealthy conditions in Chicago's meatpacking industry. The 1906 passages of the Meat Inspection Act and the Pure Food and Drug Act responded to public outrage over that industry's working conditions. Some 40% coronavirus infection rates now among employees of US pork processing plants illustrate how employers forever "economize" on workplace health and safety.

The Occupational Safety and Health Administration (OSHA) within the US Department of Labor was established in 1970. It sought to add more systematic federal government supervision and inspection to the regulations pressing employers to provide safe and healthy workplace conditions. Its mixed successes attest to the lengths employers will go to evade, weaken, or ignore efforts to enforce workers' safety and health.

The profit-driven logic of capitalist enterprises incentivizes NOT spending capital on workplace safety and health conditions unless and until they deteriorate to the point of threatening profits. Capitalists and mainstream economics textbooks repeat endlessly that profit is every enterprise's "bottom line." Profitability measures each firm's economic performance. Profits reward employers; losses punish them. Employers use capital to yield profits; that is their chief goal and priority. As objectives, workplace safety and health are secondary, tertiary or worse: obstacles to maximizing profits.

Capitalism has always sacrificed the safety and health of the employee majority to boost profits of its employer minority. That minority makes all the key enterprise decisions and excludes the employee majority from that decision-making. No wonder employers figure disproportionally among society's rich, safe, and healthy, while employees figure disproportionally among the poor, unsafe, and unhealthy. Capitalism displays not only extreme inequalities of wealth and income, but also all their derivative inequalities: economic, political, and cultural. Pandemics expose and worsen them all.

In some times and places, capitalism's iron fist wears velvet gloves. When profits are high and/or critics of capitalism ally strongly with its victims, employers may spend more on making workplaces less unsafe and less unhealthy. Otherwise, employers can and do spend less. If and when they fail to prevent government regulations mandating minimum health and safety standards, employers campaign to evade, weaken, and eventually repeal them. Employers usually repeat the same old arguments to block or undo regulations mandating safety and health standards. Such regulations, they insist, divert capital from productive uses (hiring workers) to "unproductive" uses (improving workers' health and safety). Thus fewer workers will be hired, hurting the employee class. With such arguments employers have often succeeded and undermined workplace safety and health.

Capitalism's long record of maintaining nearly constant unemployment – its "reserve army" – not only got workers to accept lower wages for fear of being replaced by more desperate unemployed. Unemployment also got employed workers to accept unsafe, unhealthy workplaces. Unemployment is a kind of torture by one class of another. It helps maintain lower wages and unsafe and unhealthy worksites. That is one reason why reduced labor needs are managed, in capitalism, not by keeping everyone employed but for fewer hours per week. That option is NOT generally chosen because firing a portion of the workforce – depriving those unfortunates of jobs – better disciplines workers to accept what they might otherwise reject.

In today's situation, employers and the government, equally unprepared for the virus, did too little too late to prevent a dangerous pandemic. Sudden mass lockdowns led to mass unemployment. Expensive reconfiguring for social distancing, mass testing, cleaning and disinfection, etc. might have rendered jobsites safe and healthy. Instead, employers and their political spokespersons press employees back into unsafe, unhealthy workplaces. A "reopening the economy" is ordered. Employers get to impose unsafe and unhealthy workplace by reframing the process as a patriotic return to a noble, national "work ethic." Employers are counting on this sham drama now.

Consider this historic parallel: capitalists in the US and elsewhere once regularly employed children as young as 5 years old. Their jobs' safety and health conditions were mostly inadequate and often deplorable. Their pay fell well below that of adults. They suffered injury as well as physical, sexual, and emotional abuse. Schooling was neglected if not altogether absent. Yet capitalists insisted that economic well-being and prosperity required their access to child labor. Ending it would bring economic decline possibly "worse" than child labor. A reasonable "trade off" was required. Employers argued that poor families needed and welcomed incomes from employed children. Employers also insisted, then as now, that they had spent all they could and all that was needed to provide adequately safe and healthy work conditions.

Working class responses to child labor took time to develop the necessary understanding and political power. Once they did, child labor was doomed. Working class parents confronted capitalists with a non-negotiable demand: overcome the horrors of child labor by ending it. Employers would have to find other ways to profit. Many did even as many others moved abroad where child labor is still allowed. They still do.

Today's parallel non-negotiable demand: end unsafe and unhealthy workplaces. That requires differently organized workplaces. The majority, employees, must control their safety and health. It must be a higher priority than profit for the minority of owners, boards of directors, etc. Once again we meet society's need for transition to a worker-coop based economy.

This article was published and syndicated by the Independent Media Institute's Economy for All project on May 18, 2020

What Happens When You Try to Save Capitalism?

May 28, 2020
Letters & Politics

Few objected to saving capitalism during its three crashes in the 21st century. We went through a kind of dress rehearsal for this 2020 crash back in 2000 and again in 2008-9 and 10. Those banks that were "too big to fail" then, are even bigger now. Many people said the steps we took then would make sure we don't have another bad crash again, yet here we are ten years later and we have it again, only worse. And sure, you can blame the virus. How wonderfully convenient. It's almost as good as blaming the Chinese. But the virus is not the problem here; it's how we coped with the virus.

After each of our three crashes in the 21st century, the US government was called on to intervene by the very same corporate executives who regularly mock the government as a monster of inefficiency and waste. Those executives begged the government to save them. And the government did: in 2000, again with more money in 2008, and now with even more money. If you put together what the US Treasury is currently dispensing to stimulate the economy (\$ 2 - 4 trillion) with what the Federal Reserve is doing (creating another \$ 2 - 3 trillion and pumping it into the economy), today's actions constitute the biggest systemic bailout in capitalism's history.

In all these cases, the Congress pushed the bills through with near unanimity. Presidents signed them. Subsequent presidents did not go back on any of them. This is considered the consensus way to handle such a crash. Only when it comes to some details (like money going to average Americans) are questions about the bailouts' affordability raised by conservatives. But all the effectively bankrupt major banks of the United States (Citibank, Wells Fargo, Bank of America, etc.) were saved with infusions of cash, grants, and loans costing trillions. The decision makers spent that money with very little concern about affordability.

The reason for this is the fast-growing perception among members of the US employer class that they are on the edge of a catastrophe, not just for them individually but for the system as a whole. That class wants the government to save it, whatever that costs. Their argument to politicians is quite persuasive: "If you don't give us unlimited amounts of money quickly, then the whole country falls apart. Don't worry about next month, next year, next decade, because if we don't get through this there is nothing to worry about. The game is over." No one should be fooled by politicians nicely dressed in white shirts and ties acting for all the world as though they have things under control. They don't. That's an act that they hope will reduce the terror all around them that this system may not make it. They are trying to convince themselves, too.

This is a grotesque injustice to the working-class majority of Americans, who are beginning to stir, and question not just this or that politician but the system as a whole. Over the last two years, the financial press has been full of the polling, particularly among younger Americans, that shows about a 50/50 split between those who prefer socialism to capitalism. The financial press is full of that because for them that's a key indicator. Are capitalists losing social acceptance of the rationale for this system that has allowed them to get as far as they've gotten? The capitalists atop the US economy want to make sure that the government they need to save them will not face the same demand from the mass of the people. The employers want the government to save them; the employees want it to save them.

The employers do not want that conflictual conversation to get going. They fear where that conversation might go. They fear that especially now, as the US enters a period where the working class will include many more victims than beneficiaries of the system.

To see where that conversation might go, we can look to our own history. By negotiating the New Deal with the left in the 1930s, President Roosevelt came up with a development that avoided fascism. In Germany, Hitler smashed the unions, killed many communists and socialists (who were previously very strong), and then constructed Nazi fascism. Germany had collapsed from the Great Depression of 1929, just like the US did, but the Germans' response was to go towards the political right with repression. The US response was to go left with a kind of social democracy. The irony is that this time the tables are turned and the opposite is unfolding.

The post WWII response to Nazism built up a powerful socialism in Germany that endures to this day. It's not a socialism like Russia has, but a socialism of compromise between labor and capital. That's why workers have those seats on the board of directors of German corporations. That's why they have a national health service. And all higher education in Germany is now free. It's not even free only for Germans; Americans can get their bachelor's degree in Germany. All these things are the results of a left that is powerful.

In the end, the great beneficiary of what the left did in the 1930s was actually the employer class. The America that came out of the 1930s, and after the end of the war in 1945, experienced the greatest period of economic growth in its history. It developed a middle class of well-paid workers who were satisfied with this system and became its supporters. This worked beautifully for capitalism. But the capitalists just didn't know their limits. As time went on, they kept pushing and pushing, until finally they got rid of the labor unions, socialists, and communists. In effect, they got rid of much of the organized US left.

Therefore, in US capitalism's very serious 2020 crash, the country has little of an organized left and so follows right-wing leaders who promise to make things great again, even as income, gender, racial, and other divisions undermine the society. But the hint in the air to the employer class is that if you don't make a compromise with the working class, if you keep imagining that you can get all the wealth for yourself, if you don't give the mass of people even what you gave them in the 1930s, you will provoke the end of your own system.

The Soviet Union didn't collapse in 1989 because anyone attacked it. If American capitalism collapses, it will likewise not be because anybody attacked it, but because the internal divisions and associated problems became unmanageable. It seems to me that anyone looking at the United States, particularly over the last 10 years, is watching the exact same USSR-style internal division and implosion literally happening as we live it.

This essay has been adapted from an appearance of Professor Wolff's on the program Letters & Politics which aired on May 28, 2020.

Is a Change in Consciousness Inevitable?

May 30, 2020
The Zero Hour with RJ Eskow

In one of Karl Marx's early works, *The German ideology*, he brilliantly talks about consciousness as a lagging reality. In other words, it takes time for settled ways of thinking to change, and to give way to new and different ways of thinking. It doesn't happen overnight. The conditions that give rise to a certain way of thinking change gradually, and when they change, they will eventually alter people's consciousness. Sometimes, it's a matter of weeks and months. Sometimes, it's a matter of decades. It takes time for consciousness to catch up, for consciousness to begin to realize that certain old ways of thinking really have to be put aside, and that we were wrong about something.

Let me give you an example of when consciousness was changed radically in a short amount of time here in the United States. During the Second World War, roughly 1941 to 1945, the United States was allied with the Soviet Union. Franklin Roosevelt, the president of the United States, had regular communication with Joseph Stalin, the leader of the Soviet Union. Russians, Russian communists, and the Soviet government and people were represented as our friends and our allies. Our enemies were the Japanese and the German Nazis. We were friends with the Russians and the Soviets. We were fighting a war together; each of us had the other's back.

Come the end of the war, and the development within a few months of a new Cold War, and consciousness had to be changed quickly and radically. The United States decided not to be allied with the Soviet Union, but to go even further and declare the Soviet Union to be the archenemy, the evil other. You had to change American consciousness quickly, so you demonized communists of all kinds, you arrested and deported the leaders of the American Communist Party, you arrested Julius and Ethel Rosenberg and put them to death, all as part of a program to change consciousness quickly and radically.

In the seventy years since then, the United States has demonized everything having to do with socialism, communism, Marxism, anarchism, etc. I can provide a personal example. I'm a professor of economics who went to the elite schools of this country: BA from Harvard, MA from Stanford, and PhD from Yale. I spent over ten years of my life in what are arguably the pinnacle of the American higher education system. During that time, no one in the economics faculties in these three universities assigned me even one word of Karl Marx's criticisms of capitalism. That's extraordinary. That's not a sign of a balanced education. It reflects ideological fear and taboo of the most dogmatic kind. My teachers were so terrified that despite having tenure (job security) they could not or dared not answer students' questions about the flaws and failures of capitalism or what the critics of capitalism had to say.

Of course, after sustained indoctrination like that for 70 years, it takes time to develop a changed consciousness.

Not that many years ago, capitalism's enthusiasts were celebrating Francis Fukuyama's *The End of History and the Last Man* and Margaret Thatcher's notion of TINA - *There Is No Alternative* (to capitalism). They conceptualized the end of the 20th century as the final, definitive victory of capitalism over socialism. Yet, in this new century capitalism has already had three major crashes. Capitalism is not secure because it has performed very badly for most people.

Let's remember that the United States represents under 5% of the world's population, and over 25% of the world's deaths from the coronavirus. US capitalism did not manage this pandemic, nor its business cycle instability, very well.

Criticisms of capitalism are rising. They were delayed by the Cold War, but that has made them no less strong or profound. The Great Depression of the 1930s was followed by huge political changes and upheavals in the United States. As a nation, we went left politically. We suddenly had a government that was providing Social Security, unemployment insurance, a minimum wage, and public jobs—15 million of them between 1934 and 41—which it had never done before.

In Germany, a country in which the Socialists were pretty strong all through the 1920s, we had equally profound political changes coming out of the Great Depression. But, a desperate business community turned to an extreme right-winger, Adolf Hitler. They made a deal with him and the country lurched to the right, further than America lurched to the left. The point is to understand that very big changes in consciousness, in politics, behavior, and in everything that matters, were the consequence of an economic crash rather like the one we're living through now.

This isn't the case in other parts of the world. The German response to the coronavirus has been, and is, very different from the American. For example, let's look at unemployment. In the United States, we have over 30 million people out of work. The unemployment rate quadrupled from

4% in February 2020 to 14.5% by April. In Germany, by contrast, the unemployment rate was 5% in February and 6 % now. There is no comparison. In Germany, the government is helping companies through the pandemic on the condition that very few are fired. US mass media go out of their way to report on this difference minimally.

Germany's business and political leaders know that if they had done what their US counterparts did—let many millions lose their jobs—they would have had immediate, mass street opposition mounted by labor unions, the Socialist and Left Parties, and probably the strong German Green Party. Germany's leaders could not keep control, so it was too dangerous to risk doing what the Americans did. The reason for the Germans' decision goes back to consciousness. In countries like Germany, France or Italy, there's a much more common and regular connection of most people's consciousness to the left. Aunt Matilda is a socialist, or Uncle Frank is a communist. Cousin Jan is a Marxist, Maria is an active trade unionist, etc. At family get-togethers, picnics, and birthdays everyone interacts with these people. If you say something offensive to the way they think, they'll probably let you know, and you will understand that things you'd say and believe have an impact on other people. If you want them to understand your position, then you better make an effort to understand theirs. Over time, you listen to each other. You don't have to agree, of course, but there's a different attitude. You understand in the intimacy of your family that there are people who think like that. You won't be able to forget it. Demonizing them will be much, much more difficult.

Many political leaders in the United States, congress people, senators, mayors, and governors have no idea what is going on here. We're supposed to believe that politicians keep their ears to the ground to make sure they're aware of what their constituents think. I don't find that to be the case. I think what has happened is that constituents are listened to, if and when they have money. Therefore, the constituents who get elected officials' ear are those who are wealthy and/or are in the business community. Those are the voices they hear. Those are the voices they talk to. Those are the families into which they marry their children. Those are the people they play golf with and go to dinner with. They will be among the last to understand when and how consciousness has changed for most people.

Thus, when a viral threat like the coronavirus emerges in a human community like the United States, the questions are how does the society respond? How does it cope? How does it manage? The answers involve preparing for and then working out a way to get through it. Fighting the virus together is actively undermined if a society is deeply divided economically, politically, racially, etc. The fact that economic inequality has worsened during the viral pandemic only further weakens the solidarity needed to fight it.

America's billionaires have gotten nearly half a trillion dollars richer over the course of this unfolding crisis. Jeff Bezos added $34.6 billion in wealth; Mark Zuckerberg added $25 billion. There is no excuse for that. It is unethical, immoral, and unnecessary. It is nothing short of perverse and obscene that the richest man in the United States, Mr. Bezos, should have become much richer while 160,000 people die and millions more are still being infected.

It is a critical time for a shift in social consciousness.

Let me remind you that it was once unthinkable to nationalize the railroads, but we did it. It was once unthinkable to nationalize an electric grid system, but we did that too. The Tennessee Valley Authority (TVA) exists to this day. The idea that we would break up or nationalize a big company because of monopolist practices is not unimaginable; it is part of American history. A change in consciousness could be further exemplified by the demand to nationalize increasingly monopolistic companies like Amazon and Google.

As enormous unemployment lingers, we're going to see the destruction of the standards of living and working for millions and millions of Americans, including those who never lost their jobs. Employers can and will cut wages and benefits because they know that desperate unemployed people will jump for such jobs if the currently employed refuse to take the cuts. That wealth being taken from them as we speak is being redistributed to the richest among us. Unless we can do something to change it, historians will look back at this moment, June 2020, and shake their heads in wonderment that there wasn't massive opposition to this state of affairs.

This essay has been adapted from an appearance of Professor Wolff's on the program The Zero Hour with RJ Eskow which aired on May 30, 2020.

There's a Crisis in U.S. Capitalism

June 9, 2020
Independent Media Institute

Capitalism has always had business cycles. The capitalist enterprises that produce goods and services are distinctively organized around the conflicted relationship of employer and employees and the competitive relationship of markets. These central relationships of capitalism together generate cyclical instability. Wherever capitalism became a society's economic system over the last three centuries, business cycles recurred every four to seven years. Capitalism has mechanisms to survive its cycles, but they are painful, especially when employers fire employees. Widespread pain (unemployment, bankruptcies, disrupted public finances, etc.) brought the label "crisis" to capitalism's cyclical downturns. Only on special occasions, and rarely, did the cyclical crises in capitalism become crises of capitalism as a system. That has usually required other non-economic problems (political, cultural, and/or natural) to reach crescendo peaks around the same time as a cyclical economic downturn. Today is a time of crisis both in and of U.S. capitalism.

U.S. economic policy now focuses on what is already the worst business cycle downturn since the 1929 crash. As data accumulate, it may well prove to be the worst in global capitalism's entire history. Forty million jobless U.S. workers find incomes lost, savings disappearing and over-indebted family finances worsening.

Today's mass unemployment also threatens those still employed, the remaining 120 million members of the U.S. labor force. Mass unemployment always invites employers to cut wages, benefits and working conditions. If any of their employees quit, many among the millions of unemployed will accept those abandoned jobs. Knowing that, most employees accept their employers' cuts. Employers will justify them as required by "the pandemic" or by what they say are its effects on their profits.

Led by Trump and the Republicans and tolerated by the Democrats' leaders, U.S. employers are intensifying class war against workers. That is what mass joblessness accomplishes. On one hand, Washington bails out employers with trillions of dollars. On the other, Washington enables (by funding) a mass joblessness that directly undermines the entire working class. Germany and France, for example, could not allow such joblessness because of their labor movements' and socialist parties' social influences. In sharp contrast, the predictable results of mass joblessness in the U.S. are

149

deepening social divisions, renewed racism, social protests, and government repression (often violent).

A desperate president fears electoral losses because his government failed to prepare for or prevent (1) a bad virus or (2) a capitalist business cycle downturn or (3) their catastrophic combination. White supremacy, police brutality, mass media control, and so on serve Trump's efforts to mobilize his political base. So do his attacks on foreign scapegoats aimed to distract blame from his government and from system failures. These include immigrants, China, the WHO, Iran, former European allies, etc.

All these tactical maneuvers by the Trump/GOP regime provoke oppositions. However, they remain dispersed and unorganized politically. Instead of mobilizing and coordinating them, the Democratic Party leadership does the reverse. It undermined the Bernie Sanders movement, especially by splitting it from a large part of the middle-income African American community. By thereby blocking, if only temporarily, a powerful emerging opposition, Democratic Party leaders deterred mass opposition to bailouts, unemployment, minimal COVID-19 testing, and all the government's other failures. They just want to win the November 2020 election. Biden's vague "return to normal" promises are offered as soothing antidotes to the Trump/GOP's crisis-wracked, fear-mongering divisiveness. Trump plunges ahead with a radically pro-capitalist agenda coupled with reactionary cultural and political warfare against civil rights and liberties. It is the old GOP strategy but a much more extreme version. The Democrats counter with reactionary responses: a revived Cold War (against Russia and/or China) and a domestic safety less shredded than what the GOP plans. Culture wars are perhaps the only realm where Democrats sense some votes in not caving further to right-wing pressures.

Alternating Democratic and Republican governments produced today's impasse. Global isolation accompanies the U.S.'s declining economic and political footprints. Its technological supremacy is increasingly challenged globally and especially in and by China. Efforts to break that challenge have not succeeded and will not likely do better in the future. Further China-bashing—pursued by both major parties—will only slow global economic growth just when many circumstances converge to make that the least desirable future. Record-breaking levels of government, corporate and household debt make the U.S. economy exceptionally vulnerable to future shocks and cyclical downturns.

The U.S. population below 40 years of age struggles increasingly with unsustainable debts. The jobs and incomes it faces have already undermined access to the "American Dream" they were promised as

150

children. Nor have they much hope for the future as today's pandemic-cum-crash imposes more hardships on them. That protests surge, provoked further by government repression, should surprise no one.

Repeated polls where half the young "prefer socialism over capitalism" reflect growing antipathy to their deteriorating capitalist reality. In the Cold War-shaped U.S. school system since the late 1940s, socialism's substantive theories and practices were not seriously taught. Debates among socialists over how socialism was changing or should change remain largely unknown. Today's growing interests in critiques of capitalism and in socialism's varieties reflect young peoples' rejection of Cold War taboos as well as a capitalism that has failed them.

No "return to normal" after the combined systemic shocks of the COVID-19 pandemic and capitalist depression is likely. Many want no such return because they believe that that normal led to both the pandemic and the economic crash. They also believe that the managers of that old normal—corporate CEOs in both their private and governmental positions—should face tough public scrutiny and opposition because of where that normal led and where it will likely lead again.

Those managers are not solving the problems they helped to create: utterly inadequate testing for the virus, bigger-than-ever bailouts for the biggest banks and corporations, mass unemployment, and deepening wealth and income inequalities.

Why then keep those managers in power? We should not expect different results from them now than when conditions were "normal."

Of course, protests flared up in and around African American communities. Beyond their long history of suffering social and employment discrimination and police oppression, it is important to remember that those communities suffered worst in the Great Recession of 2008-2009. Their unemployment then shot up, they lost homes disproportionately to foreclosures, etc. They have died from the coronavirus significantly more than white communities. Because of disproportionate reliance on low-paid service sector jobs, they have once again suffered disproportionately in 2020's crash of U.S. capitalism. When a president then blatantly panders to white supremacy and white supremacists, while making and repeating racist comments, the ingredients are in place to provoke protests. However useful for Trump/GOP electoral campaigns, social protests and oppressive police responses add sharp social conflicts to the already disastrous combination of viral pandemic and economic crash.

151

Trump is a product and sign of U.S. capitalism's exhaustion. The long, cozy governmental alternation between GOP and Democrats after the trauma of the 1930s Great Depression had achieved its purpose. It had undone FDR's redistribution of wealth from the top to the middle and the bottom. It had "fixed" that problem by reversing the redistribution of wealth and income. The ideological cover for that "fix" was bipartisan demonization of domestic socialism combined with bipartisan pursuit of Cold War with the USSR. The major GOP vs. Democratic Party dispute concerned the modes and extents of governmental support for private capitalism (as in Keynes vs. Friedman, etc.). That minor squabble got raised to the status of "the major issue" for politicians, journalists, and academics to debate because they caved to the taboo on debates over capitalism vs. socialism.

Capitalism has so extremely redistributed wealth and income to the top 1 percent, so mired the vast majority in overwork and excess debt, and so extinguished "good jobs" (via relocating them abroad and automation) that the system itself draws ever-deeper disaffection, criticism, and opposition. At first, deepening social divisions expressed the system's disintegration. Now open street protests take the U.S. a step closer to a full-on crisis of the system.

Trump subordinated the old managers of capitalism by politically threatening them with aroused, angry small businesses and middle-income workers. Trump promises the latter a return to what they had before the upwards redistribution of wealth hurt them. He tells the old managers that he and his base alone can secure their social positions atop an upwardly redistributed contemporary capitalism. They will save the old managers from Bernie, "progressivism" and "socialism." The Democratic Party's old, "centrist" leadership offers weak, partial opposition, hoping Trump goes too far and implodes the GOP.

In the wake of the pandemic and the massive unemployment used to "manage" it, wages and benefits will take major hits in the months and years ahead. Wealth will be further redistributed upward. Social divisions will deepen and so will social protests. This crisis in capitalism is also a crisis of capitalism.

This article was published and syndicated by the Independent Media Institute's Economy for All project on June 9, 2020.

Europe Fights COVID-19 Better than US

June 24, 2020
Wolff Responds

I want to talk briefly about the stark difference between the rise and fall of coronavirus infections in Europe, and the rise and non-fall of the infections here in the United States.

Europe can reasonably claim to have suffered badly but to have now driven down infections to a very low rate. The United States cannot claim the same because it hasn't. While it is correct to say we could have and should have done better, I am more interested in exploring what might explain the difference between the European experience and the far-worse US experience.

Here are some key factors. First, almost all of the countries of Europe (and especially Western Europe) have well-oiled, well-functioning national healthcare systems. In Europe, you are medically insured for whatever you need, whether you're employed or not. Your medical care is not dependent on your job; it's your human right. The United States does not have this and that's an important factor in covering a disease, a pandemic.

Second, the Europeans did not impose mass unemployment on their population the way the United States did. When 42 million people lose their job all at once (and it may well be more than that in the United States, many of whom thereby lost their health insurance) you are adding anxiety, worry, and economic deprivation to people already trying to cope with a viral pandemic. That's not going to make the situation better. Europeans did not do that.

Germany's unemployment rate in March, at the beginning of the pandemic, was 5 percent. Today, it's 6 percent. About 200,000 people lost their jobs in Germany. In comparison, the United States went from 4 percent to roughly 14 percent. Our unemployment more than quadrupled yet Germany's barely went up. The German government bailed out employers, but on a condition that they kept workers in their jobs.

The Germans have had a powerful Socialist Party for a century that has sometimes shared governing with the conservative party of Angela Merkel. They also have an important party, *Die Linke*, to the left of the Socialist Party. They have a strong labor movement. They have a law that the labor movement and the Socialists got through in Germany called *Mitbestimmung*, usually translated into "co-determination," which says that any enterprise with more than 2,000 workers must give 45 percent of the seats on a board of directors to elected workers. Workers elect the members of the board. If you're smaller than 2,000, I think 30 percent of the board of directors is elected by workers. Workers have their own representatives on the board of directors so they wield real power in those decisions, they are informed about what the company is going to do.

This means that their working-class has something that we don't have here. They have protection. So Germany addressed the changes in work due to the virus, but they did not address it by firing millions of people. That simply was not an option. The social power and influence of labor unions and the political left were simply too strong.

Third, most European leaders told their people that COVID-19 was a serious threat. They were told to lockdown, wear masks and gloves, all of it. In the United States, leadership (the President, the people around him) was ambivalent. For months they said the disease wasn't a problem. It was. They said you should be careful but then said you don't need to wear a mask. They gave mixed messages at best, thereby undermining the containment of the virus.

In Europe, you were not told that it was some kind of statement of your personal liberty to ignore masks and so on. This is more of a cultural issue. It is understood in Europe that you're not free to do whatever you want if it hurts other people. If you have the disease - with or without symptoms - you can hurt other people by not wearing a mask. This is a straightforward understanding of what it means to be part of a community and not to imagine yourself as Robinson Crusoe on some island all by yourself.

The fourth factor I would like to bring up is that Europe is a much less unequal society than the United States. The distance between rich and poor is less inside most enterprises and in society as a whole. Having a vast number of people in economic difficulty (where the United States stands out) is not conducive to a successful beating of a viral pandemic.

Finally, we have authoritarian leadership in the United States. I was struck by another statistic from the Johns Hopkins University group that is tracking the coronavirus. They listed the four countries with the largest number of people infected already, and here they are: 1) The United States, 2) Brazil, 3) Russia and 4) India.

What do those four countries have in common, besides having terrible problems with the coronavirus? Each of those four has an extremely authoritarian government: Trump, Bolsonaro, Putin, Modi. The four leaders are known for their arrogance, for their quasi-dictator wannabe attitude toward government. This could be a coincidence, but it might well not be.

We are paying the price for not having decent leadership, levels of equality in our society, or a national health insurance system. We are paying a heavy price for what we don't have and what the Europeans do have. It is something to think about because it's a very serious fundamental critique of American capitalism.

This essay has been adapted from "Wolff Responds: Europe Fights COVID-19 Better than US" which was posted on Professor Wolff's YouTube channel on June 24, 2020.

The Pandemic's Lesson About Capitalism

June 29, 2020
Economic Update: The Pandemic's Lesson About Capitalism

The coronavirus pandemic is teaching us a lesson about capitalism. We know that there was inadequate preparation for, and inadequate coping with, that pandemic. It wasn't profitable for private enterprises to prepare adequately for, and contain, this crisis. The US government might have compensated for the failures of the private profit system—capitalism—but it did not. I don't think that's an accident and I don't think that's the particular responsibility of this or that politician. That is a systemic problem.

Governments usually support, reinforce, and share the same ideology as the people in societies who run the economic system, and the United States is no different. In the case of preparedness for COVID-19, the government did not step in to do what the private sector did not find it profitable to do. This was because that would have cost the government much money, and that might have required taxing some people more. The government is also ideologically committed to celebrating the superiority of private enterprise; it does not want to be seen and exposed as compensating for major failures of the private capitalist sector.

So, what is the lesson that the COVID-19 pandemic can teach us? There are all kinds of fundamental, basic things in a society like ours that need not be, and should not be, handled as private-profit enterprise activities. That's what we learned during the pandemic. Let's explore what qualifies as a basic social need that we cannot rely on capitalism to meet, because—just as it failed to do with the coronavirus pandemic—it won't and it can't. My point here is not that you agree with the specific details of each of the following. The point is to look at how each need is currently being handled and see how we could and should do it better.

1) Health.
We know—unless we are really deluded—that there was inadequate preparation and inadequate coping with the pandemic. We didn't have the tests, the masks, the ventilators, the hospitals, the beds, the gowns, and so on that we needed. We didn't produce them, stockpile them or distribute them. Our already broken healthcare system is so costly that avoiding the doctor, even when you're sick, is normal behavior. All of this helped this virus take hold.

The government and private sectors weren't prepared and didn't cope with the coronavirus well or in a timely way. The result is an enormous loss of life and permanent health impacts for those who survive. As an economist, I also have to tell you that the wealth lost by the coronavirus pandemic is many times larger than what it would have cost to produce and/or stockpile all of the equipment that might have made us ready.

2) Food.
In the United States, we have a two-track food system. One kind of food is carefully produced with no pesticides, insecticides, herbicides, etc.; it is arguably better for you. The other kind of food is mass-produced, using every kind of chemical fertilizer you can name. I don't think this two-track food system is acceptable, and I invite you to think about it as well.

If it's healthy to have organic food, that's the system we ought to have for everybody. Do we care that other people are healthy, not just ourselves? Of course, we do. If not out of decent morality and ethics, then because we don't want fellow citizens to get sick, because the sickness may be infectious, mightn't it?

You know what the reason is that organic food is more expensive? Because of the profits involved, not just the costs. Are we going to let profit determine that the mass of people eat food that is not good for you? Food is fundamental, without it we die. Therefore, we ought to have the best food we can as a nation. We know how to make good, healthy food. That ought to be the top priority just like public health. That means we don't let food be produced only because it's profitable, because you can make profit by killing off the weeds with one chemical and the insects with another chemical, and artificially stimulate the growth hormone with another chemical, and so on.

Either we put health and healthy food as our highest priority as a nation or we don't. If we had a commitment across the food industry, we could mass produce good, healthy food. You only have to question profitability, and reorient our top priority: proper food or the profit of the food companies.

3) Housing.
One of the most basic things a society owes to the people who live in it is shelter that is warm in the winter, that keeps you from the rain, that gives you a place to recoup yourself at the end of your working day, and that gives you a place to raise children. Housing in this country is held hostage by the housing companies. They only build houses if it's profitable. They'll tell you that. There's no secret here. Is it really acceptable that we have houses not built, because it isn't profitable, while we have thousands of

homeless people who have no place to call home? We are prioritizing what's profitable and not what we know to be the moral, ethical, and socially useful thing to do. You don't build a community, a sound society, if some people have six homes and other people have no home at all. That creates tension and conflict. That's explosive; if not now, down the road. What kind of legacy are we leaving to our children?

4) Education.
Either we believe our society is better if people are better educated or we don't. Do you want to leave education to questions of profit: profit-driven colleges, profit-driven high schools, elementary schools, and daycare centers? That's what we have now: a public sector, squeezed and contracted, and a private-profit sector that is unaffordable to most. That's not good enough if you're honestly committed to education.

5) Mass transit.
As a matter of our national identity, we ought to have a high-quality system of airplane travel, train travel, street railway travel, buses, and even (at the lowest priority) private automobiles to meet our short and long-distance travel needs. We should have a mass system of transport available, staffed by specialized people who make sure that the transport is clean, safe, properly insured, that the drivers are vetted, etc. Instead, we have a transportation system mostly driven by profit.

Let me quote Donald Trump. When he was asked why he wanted workers to go back to work in the middle of the coronavirus pandemic, he said, "You look at automobile accidents, which are far greater than any numbers we're talking about. That doesn't mean we're going to tell everybody, 'No more driving of cars.' So we have to do things to get our country open." Put aside the grotesque immorality of such a remark for a moment, because it teaches us something. Mr. Trump is right: We don't, as a society, question, stop, or limit the private automobile even though it is an incredible pollutant and it kills thousands of people a year. Why do we not question this? The answer is the private profit of the automobile industry that has dominated the American economy for the last century. We could have a transit system that pollutes and kills less, but profit dominates us and so the public service of a good transport system keeps eluding us—but it needn't, and it shouldn't.

6) Care for the elderly.
We have thousands of nursing homes that are run as for-profit enterprises. The stories coming from many of them are so horrific that millions of Americans will not put their elderly in such an institution, because they know what the profit drive does to how they are cared for. If we want

elderly people to be treated decently, elegantly as they deserve after a lifetime of work and raising a family, then we cannot leave it in the hands of private profiteers.

7) Energy.
Everything depends on energy: oil, gas, sun—all of it. It should be organized to meet our needs for energy without destroying our planet. That task can't be left in the hands of private profiteers who have done everything to cut corners, to postpone anti-pollution activities, to ignore the criticism of fossil fuel dependence, and so on. If we don't want energy to be a threat to our survival, it has to be handled in a collective, direct way, not held hostage to private profiteering.

8) Military.
My last example is chosen to tell you about something which is already handled without allowing the profit motive to govern it. We do not have a military or municipal police force organized as multiple profit-driven enterprises competing for our business. Because we want security and public safety provided without regard to bottom line profitability, the government is the sole buyer of the requisite inputs and delivers the output to us as a "free" public good. We could do likewise with public health, food, and so on.

It's a reasonable demand, but it also applies to our food, our housing, our transport, and all the rest. Public health was the lesson that the coronavirus pandemic showed us: You cannot leave these things in the hands of private profiteers. As the private companies will tell you, "Profit is our bottom line." That's what the system rewards them for producing, and the system punishes them for doing what may be socially useful but is not privately profitable. That's the way the system works.

The lesson is that we have to take the things that are more important to us than private profit like our public health, our housing, our schools, our transport system and so on, and free them from the profit motive. If we learn that lesson, then the pandemic will have left us a positive legacy, not just a memory of how hard and deadly it was.

I want to conclude by asking you to think with me about what an economy might look like if it took this seriously, and how would it be organized if not for private profit? Worker cooperatives should produce all of these things: schools, transport facilities, housing. The worker co-ops would make decisions, but not alone. They'd have to make decisions together with the customers they serve and the communities in which they carry out the production. Three partners make the decision: those who do the work, those who consume the output, and those who live in and around where the production takes place and who, therefore, have to live with the consequences. These three partners all have real, concrete interests that must be represented so that the best decision for all emerges.

In this scenario, there is no place for the private profiteer—the person who comes in serving a tiny number of owners or major shareholders who want profit out of it. Would there be room for capitalists elsewhere? Perhaps they can work on non-basic needs such as restaurants, personal services, luxuries, etc.

This would give Americans the freedom of choice they don't have now. We would see how worker co-ops work in the basic industries of our society, and we would watch how capitalist enterprises work in the other less basic areas. We would see how they work differently, how it feels to work in them as a worker differently, and what the quality and quantity of output is. That would make us an informed community that could decide in the future if we want more capitalism or less. If we had an alternative all around us working to meet our basic needs without being held hostage to profits, we could make an informed choice about the different economic systems we want to produce the goods and services that a modern advanced society needs, deserves, and can actually produce. That's a way forward.

Let's learn from the failures made during the coronavirus pandemic. Let's handle the basic needs we have as a society in a way that will be successful and will not be interfered with by a capitalist system that puts the priority somewhere else—namely on profit. Profit is not always our absolute number one objective. To believe that is to be a dogmatic economic fundamentalist.

This essay has been adapted from "Economic Update: The Pandemic's Lesson About Capitalism" which was published on Democracy at Work's YouTube channel on June 29, 2020.

Part V

System Change is Underway: Which Side are You On?

Beyond the Minimum Wage Debate: Let's Move Toward a System That Works for All

July 27, 2017
Truthout

Once more with feeling, the old debate rises into the headlines and the talk show circuit: Should governments — state, federal or local — raise the minimum wage or not? Employers of minimum-wage workers weigh in to say "no." But that raises a PR problem: It looks bad to advocate keeping workers' wages so low. So, they make a better-looking claim: that raising minimum wages causes some employers to fire low-paid workers rather than pay them more. Their opposition to raising minimum wages then morphs into an advocacy for low-paid workers to keep their jobs.

Workers and their allies mostly take the bait. They weigh in with counterarguments. These mostly respond directly, claiming that raising minimum wages does not lead to significant job losses.

Over the decades, professional economists and statisticians (increasingly overlapping sets) have entered the debate. Their entry resolved nothing. Every few years, the debate has flared up again. The economists write articles and books that enrich their resumes. Some score research grants from foundations, business lobbies and labor groups to prepare shiny new versions of the old arguments.

On the level of theory, it boils down to a simple idea: If the cost of hiring workers rises, other things unchanged, the hirers will employ fewer. To this simple idea, the other side counters with another: other things unchanged never happens. For example, they point out that raising the minimum wage increases employed workers' incomes and thereby their purchases. And that means more jobs. This "income effect," they say, will offset whatever job loss higher minimum wages might entail.

Of course, lots of other things also change while (and after) minimum wages are raised. Those changes, too, will have all sorts of effects on employment. There are way too many influences on jobs to know — let alone measure — them all. But none of the players in these debating games want to hear that. There are always economists and statisticians offering, at reasonable cost, yet another study that will, they often promise, finally prove "decisive."

Empirically minded economists, adept at statistics and their manipulation, have also seen an opportunity. While theory may not resolve the issue, turning to the facts surely will, they say. They promise that looking at actual, real-world outcomes — what happened to jobs when minimum wages have been raised in the past — will settle the issue. Both sides in the debate have deployed empirical as well as theoretical arguments for many decades.

Sadly, empirical studies proved as indeterminate as theoretical ones. To pick any historical example of a raised minimum wage and then examine how employment changed subsequently runs into the problem of whether other things are unchanged again. To calculate the effect of a raised minimum wage on jobs, you must identify and exclude the influence on jobs of everything else going on when (and since) the minimum wage went up. And "everything else" is an infinity. No one can identify and measure all of the other influences exerted on a society during the time of a minimum wage change. Thus, we can never be sure that, in any given scenario, whatever happened to jobs after wages went up was an effect only of the wage increase rather than an effect also of "everything else" going on when and since wages rose.

Conservatives and employers finance, publish and circulate economic "analyses" (theoretical and empirical) to claim that raising the minimum wage will cause poor workers to lose jobs. Liberals do the same with labor unions, sympathetic religious organizations and civic groups to support economic analyses that claim no job effect from raising minimum wages.

The conservatives usually have far more money to buy and promote their analyses. Because they provide more financing to political parties, candidates and lobbying efforts, they make their "arguments" better known and are more effective in generating laws and regulations.

What actually happens to minimum wages depends little on these endlessly recycled arguments. It depends much more on the strengths of the two sides, capital and labor — what resources each devotes to shape politicians' and public opinion. For example, the US federal minimum wage today is $7.25 per hour, down from $8.68 per hour, its historical high in 1968 (measured in 2016 dollars). Across the last half-century, as the wealth produced in the US grew dramatically, cutting the real minimum wage 16 percent contributed significantly to the nation's growing inequality of wealth and income.

What we need is not another recycling of inherently unprovable claims. They have not worked to serve the interests of US workers in having decent jobs and incomes. Quite the opposite.

The endless minimum wage debate has been a distraction. Our real political and economic choice is not whether to raise the minimum wage and risk some unemployment or to secure jobs by foregoing wage increases. Consider a parallel scenario: A mugger in an alley offers you the choice between suffering a stabbing or a beating so he can secure your wallet. Will you then agonize and debate over which offered option to choose? Rationality suggests otherwise. Why not refuse both and pursue a total alternative — an escape from the alley, an attempt to disarm the mugger, an appeal to the mugger's conscience — that is far more in your interest than either option offered.

So, it is with the minimum wage debate. It represents a kind of irrationality. Economists and others in solidarity with the laboring majority should be refusing further rounds of that debate. Instead, they should demand and pursue an economic system that provides both full employment and decent incomes, and support for those who cannot work. That is the only system that deserves our backing.

This article was published in Truthout on July 27, 2017

Republicans and Democrats Are Wedded to Capitalism. Americans Deserve Better.

January 3, 2019
Huffington Post

When college student Trevor Hill stood up at a CNN town hall in 2017 and asked House Minority Leader Nancy Pelosi (D-Calif.) if her party might move further left to mark a starker break with right-wing economics, her answer was clear: "I thank you for your question but I have to say we're capitalist. And that's just the way it is."

No major Republican has felt a similar need to affirm loyalty to capitalism; everyone quite rightly assumes it. Yet the two major U.S. political parties' shared celebration of capitalism raises basic questions about U.S. society that deserve more attention than they get.

Capitalism's fundamental political problem is its class division between a small number of people who are employers and the majority who are employees.

Capitalism's cycles between good and bad times, as well as the inequality it produces through vast gaps in income and wealth, cause conflict and division. And these tensions threaten the whole system, as the recent "yellow jackets" mass movement in France demonstrates. There, a fuel tax rise sparked weeks of protest across the country as those who live beyond France's wealthy urban centers rejected — occasionally violently — yet another rise in their cost of living and demanded growing concessions from French capitalism.

In response, employers have built political alliances with some parts of the employee class. For example, inside the Republican Party, they worked long-standing deals with evangelicals to, for example, oppose abortion and coalesce around Supreme Court nominees, while inside the Democratic Party, they made alliances with large groups of religious and ethnic minorities.

They have had to make these and many more such political alliances because they are simply too vulnerable to go it alone. Their alliances' goals always included making sure that the capitalist system itself survived, partly by preventing the majority from voting for tax and regulation policies that would undo the inequalities and instabilities of capitalism.

Despite its socially destabilizing business cycles and income inequality, U.S. capitalism has been able to reproduce itself. This was achieved through the employer alliances constructed within both major political parties.

The aim of the Republicans is to identify and appeal directly to segments of the majority that feel aggrieved or threatened by certain social trends. In the U.S., this has meant appealing to, for example, white people facing the decline of white supremacist and racist practices; men seeing their dominance lessen over women at work and at home; and religious people facing the rise of secularism or disinterest in religion.

It's a gathering together of conservatives fearing the changes that are undermining old social positions and privileges. Its appeal is simple and clear. Vote for the GOP to have the government slow, stop or reverse those trends. The party always links that appeal to a rigid commitment to preserving and strengthening "the economy." By this they mean private property, markets and businesses where a dominant class of employers rules over employees.

The Democrats' mode of alliance is to appeal to the entire class of employees by endorsing state programs of mass economic, social and cultural support. For example, through subsidized higher education, unemployment insurance, Social Security increases and so on. The Democrats' plan is to pay such programs' costs by means of taxes imposed partly on employers and partly on employees.

These state programs are pitched to employers as relatively inexpensive ways of preserving and strengthening a social solidarity that includes and so supports capitalism. The programs are pitched to employees as benefits flowing from the capitalist economy if and when they have voted to put the government in Democratic Party hands.

The Democrats have generally built alliances with those segments of the employee class who most need government support (those paid below median wage and salary levels) and with those who welcome those social trends such as secularism, urbanism, diverse sexuality and immigration that upset the people who the Republicans target for alliances. The so-called culture wars in the U.S. both reflect and reinforce the class alliances constructed inside the two parties.

Both parties push "partnership" between employers and employees as an essential goal, while accusing the other party of threatening or undermining that partnership. Both also get the bulk of their funding for pursuing these political goals from capitalist employers. Donations from employees make up a much smaller proportion of their funding.

Whichever party wins, it's capitalism that prevails. The statements and activities of the party in opposition serve to funnel disaffection with the party in power into votes for regime change. Capitalism is kept out of the debates, gets a critical pass and remains secure.

It also blocks possibilities for more than two parties. The GOP and Democratic Party have together produced and sustained the rules that make third parties difficult to start or maintain.

In many other capitalist countries, it was not possible to limit political parties to two. In France, Germany and beyond, while there are center-left and center-right parties similar to the Democratic and Republican parties in the U.S., there are also politically significant parties further to the right and left. In France, for example, the National Front is a powerful rightist party led by Marine Le Pen, while the La France Insoumise ("France unsubdued") is a powerful leftist formation led by Jean-Luc Mélenchon.

In several European countries, green parties are also important. In Portugal and Luxembourg, green and anti-capitalist socialist parties are components of government coalitions. Democracy in all such countries reflects people's demands for freedom to choose among parties with divergent attitudes toward capitalism. In contrast, the U.S. — the nation that most loudly and routinely proclaims its commitment to democracy — rigidly restricts its political parties to two that both celebrate capitalism.

Modern party politics has its contradictions. By its growing dependence on major donations from corporations, it risks exposing its class nature. Failures of major parties to solve key social problems increasingly provoke people to turn against the party system. Contemporary movements for social change are increasingly skeptical of allying with any existing political parties.

France's "yellow jackets" movement — successful in defeating President Emmanuel Macron's attempts to introduce taxes that disproportionately hit those least able to afford them — illustrates that skepticism perfectly.

Similarly, the entry of Elizabeth Warren into the 2020 presidential primaries — like Bernie Sanders' effort in 2016 — moves in the direction of politically mobilizing the increasingly broad social disaffection with capitalism. Time will tell whether U.S. conditions make that direction sustainable within a changed Democratic Party or only outside it.

There is an emerging sense that new and very different parties are needed, parties that gather many segments of the employee class for a confrontation with all those who explicitly or implicitly accept and support capitalism.

This article was published in the Huffington Post on January 3, 2019.

#MeToo & Coronavirus: System is Key

March 30, 2020
Economic Update: #MeToo & Corona: System is Key

Today I want to analyze the Harvey Weinstein and #MeToo movement situation on one hand, and the response to the coronavirus on the other, because they share the same lesson: we have a systemic problem.

Sexism, a systemic rendering of the female portion of our population into a subordinate, secondary position, and the sexual harassment of women which follows from that subordination, is very old; it is rooted in long-lasting cultures and religions. Weinstein is just one example, and it is important to understand the underlying systemic problem that was exposed by the Weinstein case and by the #MeToo movement surrounding that case.

In slavery, masters didn't just oppress slaves, they also sexually abused them. In feudalism, lords not only oppressed serfs, they also sexually abused them. Then capitalism came into the world promising liberty, equality, fraternity, and democracy. That's what the American and French revolutions claimed they were for. Yes, they wanted to get rid of feudalism, and replace it with capitalism, which they did. But the values that were supposed to accompany that change did not follow. What capitalism did was to replace the top–down hierarchical inequalities of slavery, feudalism, and monarchy with a new one, namely the hierarchy of employer and employee. That was and still is the crucial systemic problem.

How does this affect Weinstein and the #MeToo movement? Harvey Weinstein and people like him may have severe, personal psychological/sexual problems. They are in need of professional help — no question. As they went about acting out their issues, they did horrible things. But it was the system of capitalism that enabled a long-lasting oppression and put them in position to sexually harass and even rape.

The employers — a small minority within enterprises — have power over the employees — a huge majority within enterprises. In terms of power, this situation is, quite like the master-over-slave, feudal landlord-over-serf, and king-over-subject, emblematic of unequal power struggles. The employer may deprive the employee of the job, the work, and the income. This could affect the employees' self-esteem as a job holder contributing to a community. The employer also has a second extraordinary power — the power to determine whether the employee is promoted. Additionally, if the employer abuses the employee, the employer can — and normally does — use the profits obtained from those workers' labor to offer them a bribe called a nondisclosure agreement (an NDA), to buy off their suffering. In this way, the employer avoids being exposed, then moves on to the next person, doing it all over again.

What enabled Harvey Weinstein, Bill Cosby, and many others to sexually harass huge numbers of people, was a system that allowed them to impose their will upon others at the cost of their suffering.

There is a parallel to be made in the US response to the coronavirus. Why was the United States so remarkably late in addressing this problem in a systematic way? Why does it represent such a failure that our nation and our leading authority, the Center for Disease Control, already knew early in January what the results of the spread of this virus were in China, but did nothing to mobilize until mid-March? By that time, not only had we seen the devastation in China, but also in South Korea, Europe (particularly in Italy), and in the Middle East (particularly in Iran). The late response had to do fundamentally with our capitalist system. This is another lesson for those open-minded enough to learn it — that we are overdue for system change in the United States.

Our medical system in the United States is a capitalist business. People go into the business to earn a profit. Doctors in their practices want to make more money than it costs to operate the practice — that's profit. Hospitals want to earn more money than it costs to maintain their institution — that's profit. The companies which make drugs or medical devices, such as test kits, want to make a profit, too, just as the insurance companies giving you a policy to cover your medical needs.

For them, the government is a danger. Why? Because the mass of people, with our right to vote, are likely to want a government that does these things for less, as the government doesn't have to make a profit. That is the difference. The private enterprise is a profit-driven business, and the government is a public service-driven organization. At least that was always the idea. So, the private sector fears government competition because the government doesn't have to charge prices high enough to earn a profit, whereas private business does.

That's the root of it — private business. However, if private enterprises were to point out that the government could do it at a lower price than they do, we all would draw the conclusion they fear most: "Well, then let's have the government do it."

So instead, the private medical sector demonizes the government, declaring, "The government is inefficient. The government is venal. The government is full of political crooks." This story is effective and contributes to the hobbling of our government. The business community and the medical business support politicians who say: "Let's keep our private medical system. Let's not have socialized medicine. If we had the government do it, it would be socialism, and socialism is inefficient and ineffective." I won't bore you by reminding you that virtually every other advanced industrial country has chosen and kept their nationalized health system. We, the United States, are the odd country out. This is the power of the medical industrial complex here.

We pay more for medical care — doctors, hospitals, drugs, devices, and medical insurance — than any other country on Earth, a lot more. That's why Americans go to Canada for their drugs. That's why an increasing number of Americans go abroad for their surgeries. The medical industrial complex makes a fortune by being a monopoly, and that is why they don't want competition from a government doing it for cheaper, just the way they do in all those other countries.

Private companies have no incentive to produce test kits and store them in a warehouse for years before there's a crisis because it isn't profitable. A government, on the other hand, could surely buy and store these items, but a government that has been infected by the profit mentality and controlled by the profit-makers, doesn't want to become involved like that.

This is why we are failing with the coronavirus. Without a centralized, government-run health system, we are unable to mobilize in the way necessary to perform the needed testing, lockdown, and quarantine to prevent the spread of COVID-19. What the coronavirus needs is the mobilization of all of our resources. This is, by the way, what has happened in China. If you don't like that example, take South Korea. They mobilized their people and by mid-March, their numbers were already much better than those of countries that didn't do this. The US needed a mass mobilization, but we don't allow our government to manipulate and control private enterprise, because we have led ourselves to believe that this would be inefficient.

Capitalism's inefficiency is exposed when one realizes how much less it would have cost to adequately prepare for and contain COVID-19, rather than the amount of wealth lost when the system could not do that.

What's the bottom line here? We have allowed a tiny number of people to have extraordinary power and wealth under their own control. Have they used it against their employees in a sexually humiliating way? Yes, they have. Have they used it to control our systems of governance in a way that further secures their profits and power? Yes, they have.

Capitalism is stumbling all over itself. It is proving that it isn't good for the mass of people, and it has made a mess of this. We can become as angry at Donald Trump as we want — he's just the presider over a system that isn't working. He is certainly not the only failure here. We may become angry at Harvey Weinstein and Bill Cosby, and we would have plenty of reason to be. But unless we change this system that supports profit as the bottom line for the people in charge of what is keeping us healthy, and allows the exploitation of those at the bottom by those at the top, we're not going to solve the now-exposed failures of capitalism to protect the mass of people.

Suppose we had an economic system that was different, which didn't have private profit as its goal. Suppose workplace decisions, including hiring and firing, promotion, and the use of profits, were all made democratically, with everybody in the workplace having one vote equal to everybody else. In this scenario you wouldn't have the lives, incomes, and jobs of the majority in the unaccountable hands of a minority. There wouldn't be the employer–employee division allowing, enabling, and inviting employers with severe psychological and sexual issues to use their positions to cause the damage Weinstein and Cosby did, or relying on profit motives to justify the efforts of saving thousands of lives from the coronavirus.

If we don't do something about this inequality, we really haven't dealt with the problem. We may only get rid of the worst offenders, the ones who get caught. Yet we'd know that the system, which has enabled countless other people to perform countless equivalent acts (even as I speak), has yet to be dealt with. If we don't change the system, we will have failed to use the opportunity that the #MeToo movement has afforded our society, and we will have missed the opportunity to produce something good in spite of the havoc wreaked by the coronavirus pandemic.

This essay has been adapted from "Economic Update: #MeToo & Corona: System is Key" which was published on Democracy at Work's YouTube channel on March 30, 2020.

Capitalism and COVID-19 Parallels Feudalism and the Black Death

April 20, 2020
Economic Update: Virus Triggers Capitalist Crash

The coronavirus catastrophe has been met with another catastrophe: the economic collapse of alarming proportions. I want very much to focus on aspects, dimensions, of this crisis that are not being talked about by our leaders across the world and, of course, especially by the one we Americans are suffering under. And I also want to talk about aspects that the mainstream media have tended to either ignore or downplay. In that way, this program can be a real contribution, I hope, to our thinking and our acting to work our way out of this twin dilemma — a virus and an economic system that cannot cope with it.

I want to begin by focusing on how and why there is a colossal failure of capitalism, particularly in the United States — because it does vary from country to country, but particularly on the failure of US capitalism — to prepare for this viral pandemic. I want to begin by making it crystal clear to everyone that viruses are part of human nature and nature around us. We have been plagued by them for as long as there have been people on this earth. I'm going to tell you a story about one, but I could have told you many. I'm picking one because its analogies to what is happening to us in the United States today are simply too obvious to overlook.

This is a story of a pandemic related to the bubonic plague, which was called the "Black Death" in 14th- and 15th-century Europe. The bubonic plague was a disease carried by the fleas that lived on rats. It lasted for centuries, coming and going. It did its worst back in the 14th, 15th century, when it killed roughly a third of all the people in Europe at the time.

In 1900, it broke out in San Francisco, California, but the then-governor of California, Henry Gage, didn't want to let the world know about it. He denied and hid it. The federal government was afraid to reveal that people were dying in large numbers from it in San Francisco. It was only when federal medical authorities exposed the virus, isolated it in the laboratory, that it was no longer possible for Governor Gage to hide.

It really did a number on the reputation of Governor Gage, and when he ran for re-election in 1902, he was defeated by George Pardee, the new governor of California. Pardee immediately imposed a medical solution that did get rid, at least for a while, of the virus in San Francisco. It did pop up again two years later, but this time the resources and the scientific community were able to prevail over the political hustler who risked everyone's life. Gage had said it wouldn't be good for business, which was probably true, and it wouldn't be good for his re-election. It turned out he blew that away anyway. I'll leave you all to think about what that might imply for our current situation.

Preparing for a pandemic, in other words, is a no-brainer, you would think. It's like building roofs over buildings so the rain doesn't get you, because it rains. It's like building a storehouse of food resources and reserves, because sometimes there's a drought, or a flood, and you can't grow the food you need. Here, in the United States, we have strategic oil reserves – big tanks buried underground. When oil is cheap, the government buys it and puts it in there. When oil is expensive, the government pulls it out. But it's a reserve in case we need it, which can't be brought up or exported otherwise. The logic is the same.

Any economic system that wants our loyalty should have to take care of the problem of preparing. Private enterprise didn't do so in our country. Private enterprises didn't produce the masks, the tests, the ventilators, the gowns, the beds, the hospitals, because to do so isn't profitable. Who wants to make a mask and store it in a warehouse for years until we need it? Not a private, profit-driven company. Profit is how they get rewarded. So they didn't make or store these items. Our American government believes that everything that private profit does or wants is what's good for all of us – a delusion of enormous size. Thus, it didn't compensate for what the private capitalist sector failed to do. So the government didn't buy and store the equipment and supplies. In other words, capitalism failed as a system to prepare for a pandemic that we know is always somewhere on the horizon.

Here's another historical perspective that might give you a way to understand the relationship between capitalism and this virus. Back in the 13th, 14th, 15th century, we had an already weakened feudalism in Europe. The people back then didn't know how to deal with depleting soil fertility. They put crops in the same place year after year, not realizing that the yield per acre, the yield per person, would go down. Inequality between rich lords and a mass of poor serfs grew. By the time the plague arrived, people were poorly nourished, contributing to why the disease was so terrible. As historians teach us, when the disease came and wiped out a third of the feudal society, mostly serfs, many of the lords went belly up. They didn't have the serfs to produce that extra beyond the serfs' own consumption that got delivered to feudal lords as rent. A weakened feudalism was vulnerable to a terrifying disease, which further weakened that feudalism.

We have a parallel situation today. A weakened capitalism was affected by this pandemic, by the coronavirus. And the suggestion of history is that the pandemic will further weaken capitalism. But to make this point I have to show you how and why capitalism was weak when this virus hit us.

Number one: Corporations, businesses – large, small, medium – had a greater load of debt going into this virus than they had ever had in history. The reason for that is capitalism. Its three recent crashes (2000, 2008, and 2020) provoked the Fed to pump huge quantities of money into the US economy by lowering interest rates. Then, every business that had a problem (a bad investment, a mistaken choice of what to produce, tensions with workers, a failed technology) solved it the cheapest way available, which was borrowing new money at almost zero cost. Businesses loaded up on debt – reasonable and unreasonable. So when the virus hit, over-indebted corporations – called "zombies" when their profits no longer sufficed to cover interest obligations on their debts – were already in trouble.

The same is true of individual debts, for obvious reasons. Also, corporations had been sending jobs abroad for decades before the virus hit. The jobs that were left paid less, were less secure, and had fewer benefits. Those jobholders solved their problems by borrowing money, which only added to their anxiety over what could happen if they could not service their loans. Squeezed budgets contributed to bad diets, high anxieties over debts, and countless derivative conditions that made workers very vulnerable to viruses.

After the crash of 2008, the US government threw trillions at corporations. The failure to basically change the society, and thereby deal with the mounting problems, produced a decade that rendered the system even more vulnerable to the next crash, whatever might trigger it. That the trigger in 2020 was the COVID-19 virus only made a very bad situation worse.

The notion that our economy was great before this virus hit is fake. All that money thrown in after 2008 by a desperate Fed was supposed to rebuild a healthy economy. It didn't. Instead it went to the stock market, bidding up the prices to atmospheric levels that were not sustainable. And how do we know that the stock-market boom was unsustainable? Because when the virus arrived, the stock market dropped like a stone, eradicating trillions in wealth.

Our society was weakened in the face of the coronavirus, the way feudalism in Europe had been weakened when the bubonic plague hit. The

176

loss of wealth in the last month is many times more than what it would have cost us to prepare for this pandemic, to produce and store all of the materials we needed. Capitalism made disastrous, inefficient choices. We're living with the results.

This essay has been adapted from "Economic Update: Virus Triggers Capitalist Crash" which was published on Democracy at Work's YouTube channel on April 20, 2020.

Why We Need Economic Democracy

April 20, 2020
Economic Update: Virus Triggers Capitalist Crash

This is a true national social emergency. It affects all of us. It threatens all of us. If ever there were justification for a democratic response in which all of us, who are affected by this crisis, can share and participate—one person, one vote—it's now to decide how best to cope. That's the honorable, ethical, moral, democratic way to cope, but we're not doing that.

What the government has done so far is to throw, yet again, an even more enormous amount of money mostly at the business community. Whether it's the Fed making money available, cheap loans on a scale we've never seen before (counted in the trillions), or it's the passing of a stimulus law that, again, sends trillions into the economy, it's mostly going into the hands of businesses. This means that in a typical corporation, the people at the top, the average 12-15-person board of directors is making the decision of what to do with whatever the government gives to "stimulate the economy." That's not a democratic mechanism.

This is allowing a tiny group of people inside each enterprise, who are committed to its profit as their bottom line, to make all the basic enterprise decisions (like how exactly to use Fed money or stimulus funds given to the enterprise). That's a terrible mistake, which we should recognize after what happened the last time the American capitalist system crashed in 2008. Again, trillions were thrown at the business community by, again, the Fed and by the U.S. Treasury. Again, the people at the top took the money. And what did they do? Did they rebuild the economy the way it was before? Not at all. Did they put billions of people back to work in the jobs they once had? Not at all.

After the subprime mortgage crash, bailed-out businesses and banks raised the salaries of top executives and bought back their own stock in the stock market, which drove up the prices of those stocks which were owned by the shareholders of the company. That's right. Corporate executives and shareholders did with that money what was good for them. And in case you need a little provocation to be outraged, some of the money the government threw at these corporations was used by them to lobby the same government so it wouldn't impose regulations on them because of the crash. Is that the appropriate way to respond to a crisis that affects everybody? The answer is "no."

Here's what should happen in every business. There should be the creation of a new council composed of everybody who works there, even the board of directors too (we won't exclude them, not that they don't deserve it). The council makes decisions using one person, one vote—from the sweeper of the floor to the CEO. We're all in this together, and we should all be involved. This would help get us what we need and are not getting: a program to transform our economy—enterprise by enterprise—so it meets our social needs, not primarily the private profits of what is a tiny minority of corporate executives and major shareholders.

In addition, we should adopt the 1985 Marcora Law from Italy. If you become unemployed in Italy, you need not become anxiety-ridden, lose your self-esteem, have worsening psychological problems, or drink too much. Instead, in Italy, unemployed workers can collect their unemployment insurance funds as a lump sum and together with other unemployed doing the same thing, use those funds to start and build a worker co-op enterprise.

Imagine such a law that gives unemployed Americans stimulus money to start worker co-ops. Not only would it offer important, creative opportunities for the unemployed. It will also build a worker co-op sector in the US like the Emilia-Romagna region in Italy, where 40 percent of all businesses are worker co-ops. Doing that would give Americans freedom of choice: to work in and buy from a worker co-op or a capitalist enterprise.

If we don't implement programs like these, we're going to get again what we got after 2008. The same capitalism that existed before 2008, which waltzed us into the crisis of 2008-10, was then re-established afterward. It gave us this latest crash. Will we permit this craziness to repeat now?

This is a crisis from which we could learn what's wrong with the system we've had and whose needs for change keep accumulating. Either change this system, or its costs will shortly overwhelm us.

This essay has been adapted from "Economic Update: Virus Triggers Capitalist Crash" which was published on Democracy at Work's YouTube channel on March 30, 2020.

Socialism vs COVID-19: A Very Different Story

June 8, 2020
Economic Update: Socialism vs. COVID-19: A Very Different Story

What would be a socialist response to the coronavirus? This is a question that I'm receiving a lot lately and what I want to try to answer.

The current reality is that the United States is one of the richest countries in the world and boasts of having one of the best healthcare systems. However, we have roughly five percent of the world's population and we have 25 percent of the world's deaths from the coronavirus. This alone tells us that something is very wrong. It turns out that what we are suffering from is less a virus—bad and dangerous as it is—and more a system that isn't working when it comes to preparing for and managing the virus.

We are also in the midst of a class war. I've said that before and I've gotten funny stares. Now in the aftermath of protests across the United States, those eyebrows don't get raised so much. Beyond the street protests, I want to focus here on class war in its quiet, relentless forms.

Here in the United States, we have roughly, according to The Washington Post, 40 million people who have lost their jobs in the last nine or ten weeks—the time of this pandemic. That is a staggering number. It's roughly a quarter of the entire labor force of the United States, numbering roughly 160 million people. Mass unemployment is also a threat to the still employed because employers can leverage a desperate workforce to lower the wages and benefits they offer to their employees. Especially in a situation like a pandemic, the employee is a prime target for "economizing" by the employer. Put these together and the level of wages and the level of benefits is going to be cut.

The people who run the economy, the employers, are going to take care of themselves first. And you, the employee, later, if at all. Wealth will be further unequally distributed, and the inequalities we had at the beginning of this pandemic will be worse at the end. That's a class war, in which the employers are likely going to come out as winners unless the employees get together and change this story.

How would socialists have handled this better? To answer, I need to distinguish between the three main kinds of socialism in the world today. The first kind simply means that the government takes a more active role intervening in the economy. It regulates more, it taxes more, it redistributes wealth through the tax system, and it manages a social safety net. This is one kind of socialism, often called democratic socialism, social democracy, etc. There are lots of terms for it.

The second kind often goes by the name "communism." Here the government does more than tax and regulate, the government actually owns and operates enterprises, stores, factories, and offices.

The third kind of socialism doesn't focus on the state and what it does. It stresses rather a transformation of the workplace from a top-down hierarchy, in which very few people (the owner, the board of directors) make all the key workplace decisions. The transformation of workplaces into democratic communities means that all participating workers make the decisions: one person, one vote. It's no longer employer/employee, neither private nor state. It is the workers themselves who take over and operate the enterprises.

Now let's take a look at how all three kinds of socialism would have prepared us differently. We know how the first kind, democratic socialism, would have handled this because it exists in a number of countries, governed by socialist parties. Spain is governed by a socialist party, Portugal is governed by a socialist party, and so on. Here's what the socialist, regulatory state would have done. It would have purchased the masks, the ventilators, the medicines, everything that was needed to handle a pandemic. The government would have bought and stored them, made sure they were kept in proper condition, monitored them, fixed them, repaired them, replaced them as needed, so that they would be prepared when a virus hit. It's not profitable for private companies to make and store these items...so they don't do it. That's why the socialist state comes in and compensates for the limits and failures of private capitalism. A number of countries do this.

In the second case, communism, the state would go beyond regulation to run the key sectors of society. Here again, we have real life examples in many countries. One of the systems that are run by these governments is the medical system: medical insurance and care combined. A government-wide national system can likely deal with any crisis faster and better than a disorganized, atomized, private (or private plus public) system. The US private, profit-driven, decentralized medical system proved unable to gather, mobilize, and coordinate a national effort against COVID-19. If the government runs the enterprises that could make ventilators, they could decide on Monday to switch from airplanes to ventilators, from automobiles to ventilators. It took weeks of people dying before that transition was hesitantly and partially accomplished in the United States, with the government pleading with private enterprises to do so.

What would happen if you had prepared for the pandemic with a system based on the third kind of socialism, rooted in worker co-ops? In such a system, the workers are already prepared to make decisions in their best interest. It's in their own collective interest to prepare before a virus hits. There's no split in worker co-ops between employers, who want profit out of the business and workers, who want wages and safe conditions, because the same people get both the profits and the wages. In capitalism, (i.e. employer/employee systems, whether private, state, or mixed) the employers, who make the decisions are focused on profits while the wage-earners with different goals are excluded from the key decisions.

What socialists would absolutely not allow is typical, capitalist exploitation. There would be no private making, promoting, and selling of medicines, masks, gloves, ventilators, etc. at inflated prices. More importantly, a socialist system would not allow for mass unemployment that makes fighting the pandemic harder, threatens those still working with wage and benefit cuts, etc. Socialism would reject forcing workers to choose between being unemployed or returning to unsafe workplaces.

For example, in France and Germany where socialism (social democracy) as a tradition is much more powerful and socially influential than in the US, mass unemployment was disallowed. Workers mostly kept jobs and kept wages paid by the government and by employers. In a communist system, where the government owns and operates many industries, leaders would have reacted sooner and probably in a more focused, organized way (as what happened in China and Vietnam). There is always the possibility that communist leaders will behave badly or ineffectively. But at least they have the capacity to react much more quickly and in a much more coordinated way to produce what's needed to manage a pandemic, like the one we're living through.

The third kind of socialism involves a worker co-op-based economy. This is the best chance for the decision-making power of the workers. They will make safety a much higher priority than in any of the other arrangements. The absurdity of a group of workers coming back to work and risking their lives would be apparent in a worker co-op. They wouldn't hesitate the way employers do to spend the money, the time, and the energy to make workplaces safe. It's their own lives they are handling, unlike a private or state employer who wonders: "Do I have to spend money, which isn't going to make me a profit, making the workplace safe for the people who work there?"

To the extent that governments fight pandemics or other social crises by funding financial stimulus programs targeting enterprises, the difference between employer/employee enterprises and worker co-ops is stark. In the former, the money goes to and is allocated by the employers; the employees are excluded from those decisions. In worker co-ops, all workers decide democratically how to make use of the government's stimulus support.

In a worker co-op, socialist system, if there was a crisis requiring the government to bail people out with stimulus money, they would be bailing out the working class; because they would be running the businesses in a worker co-op economy. The funds would be going to the majority—the working people—those 160 million members of the American labor force grouped into co-ops that would be running the stores, the factories, and the offices. It would be a radically different way of operating and coping with a crisis, like this pandemic.

This essay has been adapted from "Economic Update: Socialism vs. COVID-19: A Very Different Story" which was published on Democracy at Work's YouTube channel on March 30, 2020.

How Workers Can Win the Class War Being Waged Upon Them

June 19, 2020
Independent Media Institute

Organized labor led no mass opposition to Trump's presidency or the December 2017 tax cut or the failed U.S. preparation for and management of COVID-19. Nor do we yet see a labor-led national protest against the worst mass firing since the 1930s Great Depression. All of these events, but especially the unemployment, mark an employers' class war against employees. The U.S. government directs it, but the employers as a class inspire and benefit the most from it.

Before the 2020 crash, class war had been redistributing wealth for decades from middle-income people and the poor to the top 1 percent. That upward redistribution was U.S. employers' response to the legacy of the New Deal. During the Great Depression and afterward, wealth had been redistributed downward. By the 1970s, that was reversed. The 2020 crash will accelerate upward wealth redistribution sharply.

With tens of millions now a "reserve army" of the unemployed, nearly every U.S. employer can cut wages, benefits, etc. Employees dissatisfied with these cuts are easily replaced. Vast numbers of unemployed, stressed by uncertain job prospects and unemployment benefits, disappearing savings, and rising household tensions, will take jobs despite reduced wages, benefits, and working conditions. As the unemployed return to work, most employees' standards of consumption and living will drop.

Germany, France, and other European nations could not fire workers as the United States did. Strong labor movements and socialist parties with deep social influences preclude governments risking comparable mass unemployment; it would risk deposing them from office. Thus their antiviral lockdowns keep most at work with governments paying 70 percent or more of pre-virus wages and salaries.

Mass unemployment will bring the United States closer to less-developed economies. Very large regions of the poor will surround small enclaves of the rich. Narrow bands of "middle-income professionals," etc., will separate rich from poor. Ever-more rigid social divisions enforced by strong police and military apparatuses are becoming the norm. Their outlines are already visible across the United States.

Only if workers understand and mobilize to fight this class war can the trends sketched above be stopped or reversed. U.S. workers did exactly that in the 1930s. They fought—in highly organized ways—the class war waged against them then. Millions joined labor unions, and many tens of thousands joined two socialist parties and one communist party. All four organizations worked together, in coalition, to mobilize and activate the U.S. working class.

Weekly, and sometimes daily, workers marched across the United States. They criticized President Franklin D. Roosevelt's policies and capitalism itself by intermingling reformist and revolutionary demands. The coalition's size and political reach forced politicians, including FDR, to listen and respond, often positively. An initially "centrist" FDR adapted to become a champion of Social Security, unemployment insurance, a minimum wage, and a huge federal jobs program. The coalition achieved those moderate socialist reforms—the New Deal—and paid for them by setting aside revolutionary change.

It proved to be a good deal, but only in the short run. Its benefits to workers included a downward redistribution of income and wealth (especially via homeownership), and thereby the emergence of a new "middle class." Relatively well-paid employees were sufficient in number to sustain widespread notions of American exceptionalism, beliefs in ever-rising standards of working-class living across generations, and celebrations of capitalism as guaranteeing these social benefits. The reality was quite different. Not capitalists but rather their critics and victims had forced the New Deal against capitalists' resistance. And those middle-class benefits bypassed most African Americans.

The good deal did not last because U.S. capitalists largely resented the New Deal and sought to undo it. With World War II's end and FDR's death in 1945, the undoing accelerated. An anti-Soviet Cold War plus anti-communist/socialist crusades at home gave patriotic cover for destroying the New Deal coalition. The 1947 Taft-Hartley Act targeted organized labor. Senate and House committees spearheaded a unified effort (government, mass media, and academia) to demonize, silence, and socially exclude communists, socialists, leftists, etc. For decades after 1945—and still now in parts of the United States—a sustained hysteria defined all left-wing thought, policy, or movement as always and necessarily the worst imaginable social evil.

Over time, the New Deal coalition was destroyed and left-wing thinking was labeled "disloyal." Even barely left-of-center labor and political organizations repeatedly denounced and distanced themselves from any sort of anti-capitalist impulse, any connection to socialism. Many New Deal reforms were evaded, amended, or repealed. Some simply vanished from politicians' knowledge and vocabulary and then journalists' too. Having witnessed the purges of leftist colleagues from 1945 through the 1950s, a largely docile academic community celebrated capitalism in general and U.S. capitalism in particular. The good in U.S. society was capitalism's gift. The rest resulted from government or foreign or ideological interferences in capitalism's wonderful invisible hand. Any person or group excluded from this American Dream had only themselves to blame for inadequate ability, insufficient effort, or ideological deviancy.

In this context, U.S. capitalism strode confidently toward the 21st century. The Soviet threat had imploded. A divided Europe threatened no U.S. interests. Its individual nations competed for U.S. favor (especially the UK). China's poverty blocked its becoming an economic competitor. U.S. military and technological supremacy seemed insurmountable.

Amid success, internal contradictions surfaced. U.S. capitalism crashed three times. The first happened early in 2000 (triggered by dot-com share-price inflation); next came the big crash of 2008 (triggered by defaulting subprime mortgages); and the hugest crash hit in 2020 (triggered by COVID-19). Unprepared economically, politically, and ideologically for any of them, the Federal Reserve responded by creating vast sums of new money that it threw at/lent to (at historically low interest rates) banks, large corporations, etc. Three successive exercises in trickle-down economic policy saw little trickle down. No underlying economic problems (inequality, excess systemic debts, cyclical instability, etc.) have been solved. On the contrary, all worsened. In other words, class war has been intensified.

What then is to be done? First, we need to recognize the class war that is underway and commit to fighting it. On that basis, we must organize a mass base to put real political force behind social democratic policies, parties, and politicians. We need something like the New Deal coalition. The pandemic, economic crash, and gross official policy failures (including violent official scapegoating) draw many toward classical social democracy. The successes of the Democratic Socialists of America show this.

Second, we must face a major obstacle. Since 1945, capitalists and their supporters developed arguments and institutions to undo the New Deal and its leftist legacies. They silenced, deflected, co-opted, and/or demonized criticisms of capitalism. Strategic decisions made by both the U.S. New Deal and European social democracy contributed to their defeats. Both always left and still leave employers exclusively in positions to (1) receive and dispense their enterprises' profits and (2) decide and direct what, how, and where their enterprises produce. Those positions gave capitalists the financial resources and power—politically, economically, and culturally—repeatedly to outmaneuver and repress labor and the left.

Third, to newly organized versions of a New Deal coalition or of social democracy, we must add a new element. We cannot again leave capitalists in the exclusive positions to receive enterprise profits and make major enterprise decisions. The new element is thus the demand to change enterprises producing goods and services. From hierarchical, capitalist organizations (where owners, boards of directors, etc., occupy the employer position) we need to transition to the altogether different democratic, worker co-op organizations. In the latter, no employer/employee split occurs. All workers have equal voice in deciding what gets produced, how, and where and how any profits get used. The collective of all employees is their own employer. As such an employer, the employees will finally protect and thus secure the reforms associated with the New Deal and social democracy.

We could describe the transition from capitalist to worker co-op enterprise organizations as a revolution. That would resolve the old debate of reform versus revolution. Revolution becomes the only way finally to secure progressive reforms. Capitalism's reforms were generated by the system's impacts on people and their resulting demands for change. Capitalism's resistances to those reforms—and undoing them after they happened—spawned the revolution needed to secure them. In that revolution, society moves beyond capitalism itself. So it was in the French Revolution: demands for reform within feudal society could only finally be realized by a social transition from feudalism to capitalism.

This article was published and syndicated by the Independent Media Institute's Economy for All project on June 19, 2020.

Acknowledgements

This book reflects the labors of many editors in the various publications that published its essays. It also benefited from the many people whose questions, arguments, and other interpretations stimulated and informed my thinking over the years. All books, articles, speeches and thoughts are collectively produced and socially overdetermined: mine just like everyone else's.

I hope this book captures something of the feeling and thinking of those who sense the meaning of this historic moment of capitalism's history and who seek basic social change as the way forward. I especially and gratefully acknowledge two major contributors to this book's production: my close collaborators in Democracy at Work, Liz Phillips and Maria Carnemolla.
-     Richard D. Wolff

The editors would like to thank Richard D. Wolff for his incredibly generous contribution in writing this book. The proceeds from the sales will support Democracy at Work, a non-profit that he founded in 2012. The organization's mission is to create media that analyzes capitalism critically as a systemic problem and advocates for democratizing workplaces as part of a systemic solution.

Professor Wolff and the editors would like to acknowledge the hard work of the following dedicated volunteers who offered their time and skills to the copy editing of this book. Their attentiveness, dedication, and insights polished and deepened its contents.

Marilou Baughman
Ann Ford
Andrea Iannone
Jake Keyel
Susan Larsen
Harrison Malkin
Grant Molen

-     Liz Phillips and
Maria Carnemolla.

About the Author

Richard D. Wolff is Professor of Economics Emeritus, University of Massachusetts, Amherst where he taught from 1973 to 2008. Earlier he taught economics at Yale University and at the City College of the City University of New York. Professor Wolff was also among the founders in 1988 of the academic Association of Economic and Social Analysis (AESA) and its quarterly journal Rethinking Marxism. He is currently a Visiting Professor in the Graduate Program in International Affairs of the New School University in New York City.

Professor Wolff also hosts the weekly radio and TV program Economic Update produced and curated by the organization, Democracy at Work. His previous books published by Democracy at Work are Understanding Socialism (2019) and Understanding Marxism (2018).

Learn more: www.rdwolff.com

About the Editors

Liz Phillips is the Co-Managing and Communications Director for Democracy at Work and has been on staff since early 2018. For the 2 years prior, she was a volunteer co-leader of a d@w Study Group in Los Angeles where she focused on content production and outreach. She obtained her BFA in Technical Theatre and Stage Management from the College of Santa Fe and in her subsequent 10 years of experience in entertainment (theater, dance, concerts, film, and advertising) she held mostly management / project leadership or creative / story-telling positions. She is thrilled to now put these skills to work advocating for the world she would like to see, increasing economic (and thus political) democracy for all through the proliferation of worker cooperatives.

Maria Carnemolla is the Co-Managing Director and Director of Media for Democracy at Work and has been on staff since 2013. She obtained her MS in Management from The College of St. Elizabeth in New Jersey. She has over 20 years of leadership experience working in higher education and nonprofit organizations. The daughter of Sicilian working-class immigrants, her passion and enthusiasm for Leftism began at a young age and continues to this day. She has served as a member of the Board of Directors of the Left Forum and is also active in her community and children's schools. Maria is deeply committed to organizing and activism that focus on fundamental system change in favor of one that puts people before profits.

About Democracy at Work

Democracy at Work is a non-profit 501(c)3 that produces media and live events. Based on the book *Democracy at Work: A Cure for Capitalism* by Richard D. Wolff, our work analyzes capitalism critically as a systemic problem and advocates for democratizing workplaces as part of a systemic solution. We seek a stronger, fuller democracy – in our politics and culture as well as in our economy – based on workers' equal collaboration and shared leadership inside enterprises and throughout society.

Democracy at Work produces the shows *Economic Update with Richard D. Wolff*, *Global Capitalism Live Economic Update*, *David Harvey's Anti-Capitalist Chronicles*, *Capitalism Hits Home* with Dr. Harriet Fraad, and *All Things Co-op*.

Democracy at Work has also published the books *Understanding Socialism* (2019) and *Understanding Marxism* (2018), both authored by Richard D. Wolff.

Each of these is a collaborative effort, and are brought to you by the hard work and dedication of a small team of workers. To keep costs low, we work via a digital office and rely on donated time from Prof. Wolff as well as other volunteer contributors. We are a 501(c)3 but operate internally as a cooperative to better embody the ideals we believe are a critical part of effective system change.

Learn more: **www.democracyatwork.info**